PROPHETIC SCIENCE
ATMOSPHERES | CLIMATES | ENVIRONMENTS

SESSION 2.0

BRYANMEADOWS

Prophetic Science 2.0

Atmospheres|Climates|Environments
Bryan Meadows

©2020, Bryan Meadows
www.bryanmeadows.com
bryan@embassychurchatl.com

Published by Embassy Advantage™

Cover Design by Jason Long

Diagrams:
Justin Hardin and Damascus Media Team
Creative Team

Editing:
Tiffany Buckner
Vanessa Hunter
Glenda Giles

Research Team:
Tiffany Buckner
Nicholas Nettles

ISBN: 978-1-7348612-0-4

This book contains material protected under International and Federal Copyright Laws and Treaties. Any unauthorized reprint or use of this material is prohibited. No part of this book may be reproduced or transmitted in any form or by any means, electronic or mechanical, including photocopying, recording, or by any information storage and retrieval system without express written permission from the author/publisher.

Although the author and publisher have made every effort to ensure that the information in this book was correct at press time, the author and publisher do not assume and hereby disclaim any liability to any party for any loss, damage, or disruption caused by errors or omissions, whether such errors or omissions result from negligence, accident, or any other cause.

Unless otherwise noted, Scripture quotations are taken from The Holy Bible, New King James Version® (NKJV). Copyright© 1982 by Thomas Nelson. Used by permission. All rights reserved.

Scriptures taken from the NEW AMERICAN STANDARD BIBLE®,

Copyright©1960,1962,1963,1968,1971,1972,1973,1975,1977,1995 by The Lockman Foundation. Used by permission.

Unless otherwise noted, Scripture quotations are taken from The Holy Bible, New King James Version® (NKJV). Copyright© 1982 by Thomas Nelson. Used by permission. All rights reserved.

Scripture quotations, marked NIV are taken from The Holy Bible, New International Version ®, NIV ®, Copyright 1973, 1978, 1984, 2001 by Biblica, Inc.™ Used by permission. All rights reserved.

Scriptures marked AMP are taken from the AMPLIFIED BIBLE (AMP): Scripture taken from the AMPLIFIED® BIBLE, Copyright © 1954, 1958, 1962, 1964, 1965, 1987 by the Lockman Foundation Used by Permission. (www.Lockman.org)

Scripture quotations, marked NLT are taken from The Holy Bible, New Living Translation, Copyright© 1996. Used by permission of Tyndale House Publishers, Inc., Wheaton, Illinois 60189. All rights reserved.

Scripture quotations marked MSG or The Message are taken from The Holy Bible, The Message. Copyright© 1993, 1994, 1995, 1996, 2000, 2001, 2002 by NavPress Publishing Group. Used by permission. All rights reserved.

Scripture quotations marked ESV are taken from The Holy Bible, English Standard Version®. English Standard Version are registered trademarks of Crossway®.

Scripture taken from the Holy Bible: International Standard Version®. Copyright © 1996-forever by The ISV Foundation. ALL RIGHTS RESERVED INTERNATIONALLY. Used by permission.

Table of Contents

Introduction VII
Mission One 9
   The Making of a Star 11
Mission Two 19
   Laws of Visibility: Bending Light 21
Mission Three 33
   Prophetic Functions 35
      Functions (Chart) 52
Mission Four 55
   Terraforming the Man 57
Mission Five 69
   Terraforming the Mountain 71
Mission Six 83
   Altitudinal Zonation 85
      The Elijah Model 89
      Legal Zoning 92
      The Influencer Model 97
      Attitudinal Zonation 99
Mission Seven 107
   Constellations 109
Mission Eight 123
   Voice Commands 125
      Prophetic Sound Barriers 131
Mission Nine 139
   Dark Matter and Black Holes 141
Mission Ten 157
   Prophetic Study Guide 159
      Memory Card 161
      Memory Card Activation 163
      Prophetic Functions Challenge 165
      Your Periodic Table 166

5.4.20
Cant Be Afraid to speak
Destiny moment
Pressure on Voice
Boldness confidence wisdom to speak Gods Word
God is A speaking SPIRIT
Each grace does something for the believer
Prophets Add to the other graces

Introduction

Global warming is presenting a generation with an entirely new set of challenges. Innovators and Inventors alike are rushing to discover new energy sources and ways to reduce humanity's carbon footprint on the Earth. One of the many ideas floating within the scientific community is the audacious dream of inhabiting other planets. While this may seem far-fetched, our resources are undoubtedly becoming more and more scarce. The human family is rapidly growing, cities are becoming more crowded, and our ability to grow resources can't keep up with the demand. We need answers. We need solutions. This is why you are reading this book; it is because God has chosen you to be a part of the solution.

I believe the situation that the world finds itself in is parallel to the church's problem. Yes, Houston, we have a problem! The church has been running on fossil fuels or, better yet, old and outdated technologies. The church is losing her energy. Leaders are tired—churches are tired—humanity is tired. Why? If any gift, grace, leader, or idea is going to thrive, it takes a suitable and sustained atmosphere and environment. Hence, why I wrote Prophetic Science: Session Two. Prophets, creatives, and entrepreneurs are creatures of climate. The right atmosphere can grow fruit, while the wrong climate can corrupt character. The first Prophetic Science was all about the basics. In Session One, we dealt with the principles of practicing and judging prophecy. In Session Two, we will deal with the habitat that grows the prophet. We will deal with everything from constellations (prophetic companies) to time Ttavel (the right decision today, can change the course of your tomorrow).

Why space? Why astronauts? Jesus told parables. Jesus used stories, patterns and pictures to more accurately teach and tell stories. Session Two uses the backdrop of space, planets, and astronauts to more accurately depict the functions, responsibilities, rights, privileges and processes of the prophetic office. There is something that intrigues me about the astronaut. They are pioneers. They must be equipped with their own atmospheres wherever they go. They go through years of study and training. They are both brilliant and brave.

Prophetic Science (Session Two) is a powerful, practical and revelatory manual for prophets and prophetic individuals who want to better understand the world and the gift of prophecy. In this dynamic guide, you will:

Learn the technologies, strategies and administrations of the prophetic!
Discover the missing link between faith and science!
Get a better understanding of the heights, depths and widths of the prophetic!

Get clarity on many of the questions you may have regarding the prophetic!
Learn more about your purpose and how you are to affect the Seven Societal Mountains of Influence!
Grow in your gifting!

Prophetic Science (Session Two) is a practical, but intensive study guide that will teach you, challenge you and engage the thinker in you! The most detailed, revelatory and information-wealthy book you'll ever read on the prophetic, Prophetic Science (Session Two) is a must-have for:

Prophets	Pastors	Five-Fold Ministry Gifts
Study Groups	Schools for Prophets	Seminary Schools
Prophetic People	Mature Believers	Intercessors

Each chapter represents a classroom, and in each classroom, you will learn the spiritual, scientific and the historic side of prophecy. After each session, you will find an activation that's designed to stretch you in the prophetic. After reading this guide, you will be astronomically wiser, and you will have more clarity regarding your assignment here in the Earth!

Mission One

T-09

Spectrum of Influence

develop people at high rate
  online platform to train strength gifts

★ A gift begins: (2)
   dust — flesh ⎫ interaction
   gas — spirit ⎭ wrestle of flesh + spirit

Get used to own season grip orbit management
   fuse ⟶ form of new elements different
                     gen 2:5-7

The sun is a star —
   Comedy EXAMPLE BASKETBALL

- dirt & inspiration (gas)
- wrestling better than this
- opener MC loosen up people
  featuer 15-20 minutes Prepare for 30
  head liner

(A few more month Apostle star
    working the altar)

hardest of core the brighter you are
every season will feel small more I do the less
   explode — to pop — I don't give A —
                     — I'm going to be me
                   the more the   Authentic
                   light shines — confidence

Every gift has it's own solar system

The Making of a Star

> "All flesh is not the same flesh: but there is one kind of flesh of men, another flesh of beasts, another of fishes, and another of birds. There are also celestial bodies, and bodies terrestrial: but the glory of the celestial is one, and the glory of the terrestrial is another. There is one glory of the sun, and another glory of the moon, and another glory of the stars: for one star differeth from another star in glory" (1 Corinthians 15:39-41).

What is a star? According to Wikipedia, a star is "an astronomical object consisting of a luminous spheroid of plasma held together by its own gravity." But before we go any further, let's get a better understanding of space as a whole. Space, while accessible to man to a certain degree, has still managed to hold on to its biggest secrets and mysteries. One of its mysteries is the sun itself. While we now know a lot about the sun, there is still a lot that we do not know. What we do know is:

1. The sun is a giant star.
2. The sun sits in the center of our solar system, but more than that, the sun is the solar system, given the fact that the mass of the Sun accounts for 99.8% of the mass of the Solar System.
3. The sun is a mixture of all colors, even though it appears to be white to us.
4. The sun is 109 times wider than Earth and 330,000 times as massive as Earth.
5. The temperature inside the sun can reach 15 million degrees Celsius.
6. The sun moves; it travels at 220 kilometers per second.
7. Light from the sun takes eight minutes to reach the Earth.
8. The sun has a very strong magnetic field.
9. Scientists believe that the sun will consume the Earth someday.
10. A third of the sun is made of hydrogen.

Hydrogen is an odorless, colorless and highly flammable gas; it is the chemical element with the symbol H and atomic number 1 in the periodic table. It is the lightest element in the periodic table, even though it is the most abundant chemical element in the universe, consisting of 75 percent baryonic mass. The word "hydrogen" comes from the Greek word "hydro" (ὑδρο-) meaning "water" and "genes" (-γενής) meaning "creator." Scientists estimate that hydrogen makes up 90 percent of all atoms found in the universe. Why is this important? About 99 percent of your body is made up of atoms. An atom is the smallest unit of matter that retains all of the chemical properties of an element. In truth, everything on Earth is made of atoms except energy. The atoms in our bodies bond together to form molecules, which make up matter. According to Google's Online dictionary, a molecule is "a group of atoms bonded together, representing the smallest fundamental unit of a chemical compound that can take part in a chemical reaction." A few examples of molecules are:

- H_2O (water)
- N_2 (nitrogen) *Most Abundant colorless odorless*
- O_3 (ozone)

PERIODIC TABLE OF ELEMENTS

On the periodic table, you'll see a list of elements. A molecule, in layman's terms, is the bonding together of two or more of these elements. When these elements come together, they react and form something, for example, water is created when two hydrogen atoms attach to an oxygen atom, thus, the formula H_2O. When any of the elements on the periodic table come together, they react, and something is formed as a result of that reaction.

The term "atom" comes from the Greek word "atomos" which simply means indivisible. An atom is the smallest unit of measure, meaning, it cannot be further broken down. What's interesting enough is that we are all made up of atoms, just as we are all made up of Adams. Of course, we all know who the first Adam is. He was the first man to ever be created by God.

He is the first atom from which we were created. Jesus Christ, of course, is the second Adam. And while He may be referred to as the second Adam, He is the basic element from which we were all created. In other words, He did not build His foundation on the first Adam, nor did He launch His earthly ministry on the first Adam.

- **John 1:1:** In the beginning was the Word, and the Word was with God, and the Word was God.
- **Revelation 22:13:** I am Alpha and Omega, the beginning and the end, the first and the last.
- **John 8:58:** Jesus said unto them, Verily, verily, I say unto you, Before Abraham was, I am.

[handwritten note: Ps 51 came through Adam's transgression sin]

Follow me into the lab to see the creation of Adam. You'll have to use your imagination for this presentation. Genesis 2:6-7 details this very event; it reads, "But there went up a mist from the earth, and watered the whole face of the ground. And the LORD God formed man of the dust of the ground, and breathed into his nostrils the breath of life; and man became a living soul."

1. A mist went up from the Earth; this, of course, is water.
2. It watered the whole face of the ground; the ground, of course, was sand. Sand and soil are not one in the same, but we'll discuss this later.

God formed man from the dust of the ground. God formed man from an element. But remember, the dust of the ground had also been watered by the mist that came from the ground. This dew allowed the dust to bond together. Without the dew, the body of the man would not have been able to take shape; it needed a bonding agent. Of course, water, in the scriptures is symbolic of purification and eternal life, just to name a few. So, God formed mankind with a natural element, and then, He bound us to eternity. Adam was pure (without sin), but lifeless. God then breathed the breath of life into Adam's (atom's) nostrils and he became a living soul.

The word "breath" comes from the Greek word "pneuma" and it literally means spirit or soul. So, what God essentially did was to bind together a bunch of sand particles, fuse them together with water, and then, He bound Himself to the mixture by imparting His own breath into what was once nothing but a pile of wet dirt. Please keep in mind that our bodies are 60 percent water, our brains are 73 percent water and our lungs are 83 percent water. Adam's body was nothing but sand and water. I think we'd all like to imagine Adam lying on the ground, naked and coughing like a newborn baby who's just entered the Earth, but it wasn't like this at all. Adam was born upright. He didn't come from a womb, he came from God (Alpha, the Beginning). His body, on the other hand, came from an element; it was created using the dust from the ground and a lot of H2O (hydrogen atoms and oxygen). It was created by God

(Omega, the End). When the supernatural merges with the natural, a miracle occurs. Adam was a miracle. A miracle, in short, is an impossibility that proves itself to be possible.

Again, your body is made up of 99 percent atoms; an atom is the smallest unit of measurement. We are made of Adams (the first Adam and the second Adam: Christ). We have our adamic nature, which is our sin nature; this, of course, is the result of Adam transgressing against God. By doing this, he added sin to the elements. Because of this, sin became a part of our makeup; it has infused itself into our DNA, and this is why we are prone to sin. When sin entered Eve, it entered her DNA. As humans, we get 50 percent of our DNA from our mothers and we get the other half of our DNA from our fathers. This means that our parents are the basic elements that came together to give us our issues. But Satan's focus wasn't on Eve. His overall goal was to contaminate Adam; this is because Adam (atom) was the basic building block of mankind. Eve came from Adam, but Adam had come from God. In other words, it is possible that had Adam remained free from sin, his sinless nature could have redeemed the children he would have produced with Eve. "And the woman which hath an husband that believeth not, and if he be pleased to dwell with her, let her not leave him. For the unbelieving husband is sanctified by the wife, and the unbelieving wife is sanctified by the husband: else were your children unclean; but now are they holy (1 Corinthians 7:13-14). All the same, even though we get 50 percent of our DNA from both parents, according to science, you are 60 percent more likely to have active traits from your natural father than from your mother. Please don't think that Satan was ignorant of this! He knew the importance of fathers, given the fact that he knew our Father, YAHWEH. So, while Eve was a bonus capture, Satan was focused on the basic building block himself, Adam. It is for this reason that he not only tempted Eve to sin, he imparted his nature into her through her sin. How so? The spiritual world works through agreements. Eve received two reports; the instructions that she would follow would determine her future.

- **God's Instructions/Genesis 2:15-17:** And the LORD God took the man, and put him into the garden of Eden to dress it and to keep it. And the LORD God commanded the man, saying, Of every tree of the garden thou mayest freely eat: But of the tree of the knowledge of good and evil, thou shalt not eat of it: for in the day that thou eatest thereof thou shalt surely die.
- **Satan's Temptation/Genesis 3:4-5:** And the serpent said unto the woman, Ye shall not surely die: For God doth know that in the day ye eat thereof, then your eyes shall be opened, and ye shall be as gods, knowing good and evil.

Notice that God gave Eve a commandment, but Satan didn't tell her what to do, he tempted her into sin. The reason for this is, he had no dominion over her. If he'd commanded her to eat from the Tree of the Knowledge of Good and Evil, Eve would not have listened to him. He needed her to involve her own will into the equation. This would bind him to her and her to him, since the basic building block of sin is called a lie. This is why Satan is called the father of lies. Satan had no legal jurisdiction in the Garden of Eden, and he had no authority over Adam and Eve. So, he tempted Eve into sin, hoping that she would become just like him; she would become a tempter herself. It worked. After biting into the forbidden fruit, Eve went and found her husband, Adam, and gave him the same lie that she had bitten into. Adam didn't ask any questions. He simply took the fruit and bit into it. The basic building block of mankind was now contaminated with sin, meaning that every child produced by him would have 50 percent of his DNA and 50 percent of Eve's DNA, which would make them 100 percent sinners.

All humans today have 46 chromosomes: 23 from each parent. When sin entered the DNA of a man, it twisted or perverted man's DNA. This is why the picture you see of a DNA strand looks like a twisted ladder. The ladder between Heaven and Earth is a narrow, straight line. "Enter ye in at the strait gate: for wide is the gate, and broad is the way, that leadeth to destruction, and many there be which go in thereat" (Matthew 7:13). The Prophet Jacob dreamed of this ladder. Genesis 28:12 says, "And he dreamed, and behold a ladder set up on the earth, and the top of it reached to heaven: and behold the angels of God ascending and descending on it." Amazingly enough, the number 23 is perceived as a symbol of death, while the number 46 is used to symbolize resurrection.

Let's look at our galaxy once again. Again, a star is a body of glowing gas formed in an interstellar cloud of dust, helium, hydrogen, plasma and other ionized gases called a Nebulae. The word "Nebulae" comes from the Latin word "cloud." How are stars formed?

1. **Clouds of dust and gas are disturbed by the gravity of a nearby phenomenon.** The Bible tells us that Adam and Eve were both naked and unashamed in the Garden, but once they'd transgressed against God, they suddenly saw each other's nakedness. Let me submit to you that the reason Adam and Eve had not been able to see one another's flesh is because they were both clothed in the glory of God, but when they sinned, the glory lifted from them. What I'm saying here is that the star (David) was created when the clouds (glory of God) and the dust were disturbed by a nearby phenomenon who, of course, was God.

2. **This disturbance causes clumps to form; these clumps attract gas inwardly.** Again, God fused sand and water together to create the Earth suits that we would wear; He created our bodies from sand and water. Please note that sand forms when rocks break down from weathering, meaning that sand is nothing but the smallest particle of a rock.

3. **The clump collapses and begins to rotate; it flattens and becomes a disc-like pattern of gas and dirt.** God breathed into the lungs of Adam and fusion began to take

place. Think of it this way. Imagine a pile of sand, formed into the shape of a man. Now imagine a ball of light and energy surrounding that man at an amazing speed, and then, suddenly, entering into the man through his nose. Suddenly, the man's eyes open and he breathes his first breath.

4. **The disc continues to increase in speed, pulling more material inward.** This creates a hot, dense core called a protostar. A protostar is a young star that is still gathering mass from its parent molecular cloud. The protostar, in this case, was Adam himself. He became a student of God or a smaller star. Before Adam could reproduce or pour out, he had to first become a student. This is very similar to downloading software to a brand new computer.

5. **The protostar increases its temperature, and when it is hot enough, hydrogen atoms begin to fuse; this produces helium and energy.** This can be compared to the moment a computer finally powers on for the first time. This is the moment that we use the computer for the first time. God brought the animals to Adam to see what he would call them. This is the equivalent of what we call beta testing; it's when a manufacturer tests out the software or program he's created for the first time. Adam, of course, passed this test, proving that he was ready to fulfill the purpose for which he had been created.

6. **The created energy forms the glow that we see emitting from stars, and thus, a star is born.** This is when a star begins to shine; this is the moment when the star emerges and is ready. Most stars have trace amounts of carbon, nitrogen, oxygen and iron in them; these elements had been created and left behind by the stars that existed before them. God is a star. He pulled Adam out of Himself, and when Adam was ready, he began to glow or, better yet, he began to emit the glory of God. This was the cloud that surrounded him. It wasn't just outside of him, but God's glory radiated from within Adam. When Adam began to look like His Creator, God pulled Eve out of him.

Adam was a star because His Creator is a star. Of course, I'm not saying this in the literal sense of the word; I'm definitely not telling you to start worshiping the hosts of Heaven. Simply put, what this means is that we are very similar to the stars in the sky. When Adam sinned against God, the glory of God left him, and like a comet, he fell from grace. The same had once happened to Lucifer. Isaiah 14:12-15 reads, "How art thou fallen from heaven, O Lucifer, son of the morning! how art thou cut down to the ground, which didst weaken the nations! For thou hast said in thine heart, I will ascend into heaven, I will exalt my throne above the stars of God: I will sit also upon the mount of the congregation, in the sides of the north: I will ascend above the heights of the clouds; I will be like the most High. Yet thou shalt be brought down to hell, to the sides of the pit."

Adam was a star. Like Lucifer, he became a fallen star. But unlike Lucifer, mankind would receive redemption through another star by the name of Jesus, who was and is the Christ. The atoms from which we were made had been perverted because of Adam's sins, but God would raise up another Adam. 1 Corinthians 15:40-49 states, "There are also celestial bodies, and bodies terrestrial: but the glory of the celestial is one, and the glory of the terrestrial is another. There is one glory of the sun, and another glory of the moon, and another glory of the stars: for one star differeth from another star in glory. So also, is the resurrection of the dead. It is sown in corruption; it is raised in incorruption: It is sown in dishonour; it is raised in glory: it is sown in weakness; it is raised in power: It is sown a natural body; it is raised a spiritual body. There is a natural body, and there is a spiritual body. And so, it is written, The first man Adam was made a living soul; the last Adam was made a quickening spirit. Howbeit that was not first which is spiritual, but that which is natural; and afterward that which is spiritual. The first man is of the earth, earthy: the second man is the Lord from heaven. As is the earthy, such are they also that are earthy: and as is the heavenly, such are they also that are heavenly. And as we have borne the image of the earthy, we shall also bear the image of the heavenly."

Prophetic Activation

List three prophets in the Bible that you can relate to the most, and detail at least three characteristics you believe that you have in common with each of these prophets. When you're finished, you should have, at minimum, nine pointers.

Mission Two

T-08

Laws of Visibility: Bending Light

While we do live according to chronos time, there are things that God does in certain seasons, and as believers, we must be sensitive, having the anointing of Issachar … the anointing of the Bereans to dig out a thing. We must have the ability to discern the seasons that we are in. When seasons change, clothes change, temperatures change and the weather changes—even weather patterns change. As believers, we must be cognizant of when God begins to change our seasons. What God does to change a season is, He rearranges or, better yet, He moves and positions light beings. Whenever seasons change, the constellations change. The moment the constellation begins to rework itself, you'll begin to see seasons change. Those seasonal changes have planetary effects; this also affects the vegetation. This literally means that when you go outside of your house and look up, the stars and their alignment have shifted based on the season. This is because when God wants to change a season, He changes the placement of stars. That's not just true in our lives, it's also true in the body of Christ. When God wants to change a season in the body of Christ, He begins to put gifts in their proper places. 1 Corinthians 12:28 says, "And God hath set some in the church, first apostles, secondarily prophets, thirdly teachers, after that miracles, then gifts of healings, helps, governments, diversities of tongues." All of this is great, but the word "set" is the word I want to highlight. He did not suggest, He set. And this particular word goes all the way back to the Old Testament when God told Moses to create the garments for Aaron the high priest. He said, "I want you to take jewels, and I want you to *set* them in the breastplate of Aaron." These jewels represent the twelve tribes of Israel. They were set; they could not be removed. Just like a jeweler can't just take a diamond and put it on your hand, the jeweler would have to set it in gold, white gold or platinum. So, when God wants to change a season, He changes the seating of the people at your table. Psalms 23:5 says, "Thou preparest a table before me in the presence of mine enemies: thou anointest my head with oil; my cup runneth over." When a scripture talks about a table, it's talking about a season. When your seasons change, the tables that you sit at change!

When He changes your table, He changes the counsel around the table. That's the level of information that you have access to; that's the level of revelation and wisdom that you have access to. God can enlarge a table. When God wants to change a season, He changes the placement of things and the placement of people. There are some people who you used to be very close with and God changed their placement or He *will* change their placement. This doesn't mean that He's going to remove them from your life; they just might not be as important as they were in seasons past. When God begins to change their placements, don't chase them; release them.

Laws of Visibility: Bending Light

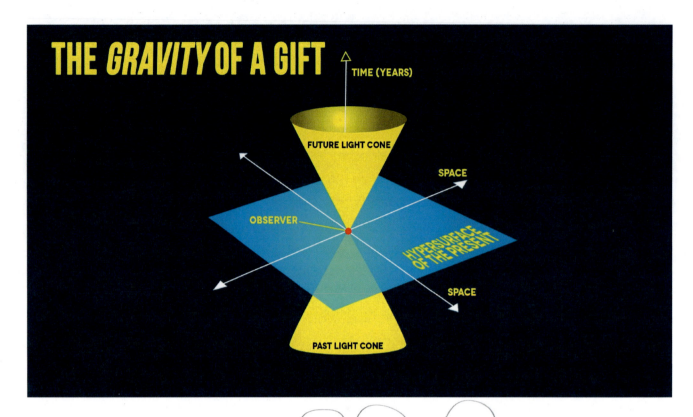

In this chapter, we are going to talk about gifts, influence and visibility. Your gift can only be hidden for so long. This is why the scriptures say that what is done in the dark will be revealed in the light. That's not always talking about sin, but when you were in your season of darkness, you were preparing, you were praying and you were pure. So, when the light comes on, you won't be afraid of exposure. You've been preparing for this; you've been praying for this! The darkness is the moment or the time of development, but light is the revelation of what you've done while in the dark. What happens when you're at the edge or at the cusp of the season that you've been praying for, and it's no longer a distant memory? Instead, it has become a reality. You can touch it, you can feel it and you can taste it—you're afraid, but you're excited all at the same time!

Genesis 37:1 starts off this way, "And Jacob dwelt in the land wherein his father was a stranger." Now, this is already a significant statement. I'll say it this way, "And Jacob was familiar in a land where his father was a stranger." The word "stranger" can also mean "sojourner" or "pilgrim." While Jacob dwelt, his father only passed through, so seasons that were like flashes for Jacob's father, Isaac, became an everyday reality for Jacob because Jacob dwelt there. Genesis 37:1-2 says, "And Jacob dwelt in the land wherein his father was a stranger, in the land of Canaan. These *are* the generations of Jacob. Joseph, being seventeen years old, was feeding the flock with his brethren; and the lad *was* with the sons of Bilhah, and with the sons of Zilpah, his father's wives: and Joseph brought unto his father their evil report."

Now, when it says "their evil report," please understand that it was the job of Joseph to tend the sheep. Joseph was a shepherd. Shepherds didn't just deal with sheep, they were also businessmen. Every businessman had to account for budgets; they didn't just watch over sheep, they watched over wool. They watched over how much milk a sheep produced and how much water a sheep consumed. The job of a shepherd was a very arduous task. You had to understand law because if the sheep grazed on someone else's field, that sheep would become the property of the person who owned that field. So, you couldn't allow a sheep to wander onto someone else's property because you could lose that particular sheep. That's why every shepherd had a shepherd's rod; it had a hook on it. If a sheep got outside of its jurisdiction, the staff would allow him to elongate his authority or influence so that he could bring the sheep back into his fold. The shepherd was very significant, especially in those days because all of their clothes were made out of wool. They wouldn't have clothes if they didn't have sheep, they wouldn't have milk if they didn't have sheep, they wouldn't have meat if they didn't have sheep. As a matter of fact, they would take the fat from the animals to make candles. In other words, you wouldn't have light if you didn't have a shepherd, so a shepherd was a very intricate part of agricultural society, so when the scripture says that Joseph was feeding the flock of his brethren, he wasn't in a slave role or a servant type role. This was a very dignified position; it was dirty, but it was dignified. It was dirty, but there was honor to it. Joseph's job was to take inventory or to give a report. I'm sharing this because I don't want you to think that he had ought against his brothers; he was just telling the truth. His brothers were doing evil, so he brought to their father an evil report.

Certain parts of the scriptures refer to Jacob as Jacob, but in other parts of the scriptures, Jacob is referred to as Israel. Whenever the scriptural text is dealing with the flesh or the humanity of Israel, it would use the name Jacob, but whenever the scriptural text is dealing with the promises, the destiny or the future of Israel, it would use the word Israel. Genesis 37:3 states, "Now Israel loved Joseph more than all his children, because he was the son of his old age." I want to highlight the phrase "old age" here. It doesn't mean that they were talking about Jacob's elderly stage. The phrase itself is a very bad translation; it literally means the son of his father's wisdom. Joseph was born out of wisdom; he was not born out of lust or desperation. He was born out of wisdom. Jacob had tried to have children eleven times; his predecessors were unable to have children. Isaac married Rebekah, but Rebekah couldn't get pregnant. Abraham married Sarai (later Sarah) and Sarah couldn't get pregnant. Jacob's problem wasn't that his wives couldn't get pregnant; they all got pregnant, but the issue was, none of the babies were the right one. You see, sometimes, your lack of productivity is God's wisdom. God knows that if He gave you everything you wanted in the wrong season, you would take that money and squander it. He also knows that if He delays your gratification, allowing you to deal with the struggles of trying to scrap up enough money to pay your bills, when you finally get the money, you'll pay off your bills and your debt. He had to delay the money until you were mature enough to handle it. Sometimes, delay is wisdom. Have you ever tried to leave your house, but you couldn't find your keys or you couldn't find something that you needed? Later on, you found out that there had been an accident on the path you were set to travel on. God wanted to delay you so that you wouldn't get into that accident.

The scripture goes on to say that Jacob made Joseph a coat of many colors. When children were born in the days of old, they had to already have a blanket or a coat made for them. This is because they didn't have heat back then, so if the baby didn't have a blanket, the baby could get hypothermia or become susceptible to disease. The baby could catch a cold, catch the flu or any of the ailments that were prevalent back then, and consequently die before its time. So, while the mother was pregnant, it was the father's job to knit what we call a mantle. This is so that when the baby came out, it would be covered—any gift in its infancy must be covered. Now, I want you to understand that Joseph was a star. He was a gifted person; he was a gift of influence. As the gift began to emerge, God knew that if he had been exposed before his time, there would be people who would try to kill the gift. If people saw your potential before your time, you would be in danger. This is why the scriptures say that the princes of this world had known who Jesus was, they wouldn't have ever crucified the Lord of Glory. So, what God does is He blinds people to your potential. You'll find yourself complaining, saying things like, "Why they don't support me? Why they don't come to my events? Why don't they buy my products?" The answer is because they're blind. It's not that you're irrelevant; the truth of the matter is, God made them blind because if they could benefit from your gift, they could get it for half off. God made them blind until your price went up! If the people around you knew how gifted you are, everybody would be calling you and emailing you asking for a discount. So, God made them blind to your potential.

Joseph's father made him a coat of many colors. Now, colors in the scriptures represented functions. In the courts of kings, you could tell or discern the function of a person based on the colors that he or she wore. So, when it says that Joseph had a coat of many colors, it literally means that his father gave him a mantle that allowed him to access many spheres of influence. Joseph had entrance into the business world, entrance into the entertainment world, entrance into the world of family, entrance into the religious world—he had legal authority to go into any sphere of influence and he was anointed to change that sphere. Joseph had a coat of many colors, meaning, he could not be boxed in. His anointing was multi-functional; his anointing was multidimensional. It was multi-sided and he was multifaceted. He wasn't just good at one thing.

Genesis 37:4 goes on to say, "And when his brethren saw that their father loved him more than all his brethren, they hated him, and could not speak peaceably unto him." One of the ways that God exposes devils is by favor. Some people that you think are your friends may only be your friends when you're broke. The moment you get money, it won't be uncommon to hear people say, "You've changed." This is what I've found out—it's not that you've changed, it's just that their perception of you has changed. And when how they perceive you changes, they'll misconstrue everything that you do. Please note that your heart is the prism that your perception sees through. If your heart is broken or shattered, you're going to see everything twisted, so the health of your heart determines the health of your perception. When people say that you've changed, what they're really saying is that they themselves haven't changed. They are watching you evolve while they remain stagnant. Your growth indicates their lack of growth.

Do you remember the story where Hannah wanted to get pregnant? She was married to Elkanah, and Elkanah had two wives: Hannah and Peninah. Peninah had gotten pregnant every single year, but Hannah was barren. Hannah went into a praying frenzy, meaning, her prayers didn't look dignified, so much so that her husband thought she was drunk. Imagine her staggering and slurring her words—she could barely speak comprehensively. She was in a frenzy of prayer. This was not a cute, dignified prayer. She kept praying for a son. Prayer is like picking a lock; intercession is like picking a lock. She finally put together the right words or the right combination code; she said, "Lord, if you'll give me a son, I'll give him back to you." So, God gave her a son. She honors her word when Samuel is born; she took the child to the Tabernacle and gave him to a priest named Eli. 1 Samuel 2:18 reads, "But Samuel ministered before the LORD, being a child, girded with a linen ephod." Now, remember that colors represent functions. Priests would wear white; it was a linen ephod. Colors didn't just represent functions in the scriptures, textures also represented functions. Fathers had to be seamstresses; they had to be makers of anointings—cloaks, mantles and garments. And through that, they had to understand the prophetic meaning of colors. If a father put purple on his son, he had to understand what that activated, or if he put blue on his son, he had to understand what that activated. And again, garments also had textures. Just a sidebar, your character is the shape of your soul and your attitude is its texture. This is why people say stuff like, "She rubbed me the wrong way." In other words, there is friction. This is because the woman in question is rough around the edges; she hasn't been smoothed out yet. Ephesians 5:26 says, "Be washed by the water of the Word." How do you smooth a hard rock? By water. How do you smooth a hard heart? By water. So, as she is seated under the Word of God, the water of the Word will soften her up.

The scriptures say that John, the Baptist, had a garment that was made out of leather and camel's hair; this is because prophets must have rough texture. Jesus asked the people, "What did you come to see? A man clothed in soft raiment? People with soft raiment are in king's palaces!" Hear me—you can't be ghetto in the White House. You can have camel hair and leather in the desert; you can preach to everyone and say whatever you want, but if you're going to go into the White House, you have to be adorned in soft raiment. This means a gentle personality.

Samuel's garment gave him the ability to function as a priest. What did his mother do? Let's read Samuel 2:19. "Moreover his mother made him a little coat, and brought it to him from year to year, when she came up with her husband to offer the yearly sacrifice." Why did she do this? Because his anointing had to grow with his character. As he was growing physically, he was outgrowing the garment that had been made for him the previous year. In other words, you have to have a covering to say what you used to fit in. You need leaders who will tell you when you're too big to fit in that last box, to fit on that last level or to fit in that last dimension! When you grow, your anointing must grow. You need someone who's monitoring your growth, and as they are watching, they're stitching. Samuel's mother made a coat for him year after year; this means that he grew. Anytime she left and came back, he was better at what he did. His skill did not stay at the same level.

When Joseph was first born, he was covered. His father saw the favor on his life and covered him. When gifts are first born, they must be covered. The word "covered" doesn't just mean to conceal, it means to protect. Why are we discussing this? Because you can be unprepared for a season that you've prayed for. You can want something, but not be ready for it when it comes. John 12:24 reads, "Verily, verily, I say unto you, Except a corn of wheat fall into the ground and die, it abideth alone: but if it die, it bringeth forth much fruit." When it says "die," it literally means to lose its will. Once you got born again, you should have died to yourself; the reason that most Christians can't function in their Christianity is because they are still alive. God can't use you while you're doing what you want. You have to literally deny yourself! Jesus told His disciples in Matthew 16:24, "If any man will come after me, let him deny himself, and take up his cross, and follow me." You have to tell God, "Everything that I've always wanted, I no longer want because I want you." That's foundational level Christianity. The scriptures tell us that when we come, we must come like a child. I'm saying that to inform you that you have to go into the ground and die to yourself. Mark 4:28 says it like this, "For the earth bringeth forth fruit of herself; first the blade, then the ear, after that the full corn in the ear." Get this—when a gift begins to crack the surface of visibility, the first thing you'll see is the blade. When the Bible uses the word "blade," it's talking about a stem of grass. This is a very dangerous stage of emergence because sheep eat grass. You have to be careful! When your gift starts to emerge in a church, church people will eat your gift up! They won't care about your character, they won't care about your finances, nor will they care about your family! All they care about is themselves. Hear me—a blade can't handle weight! As a matter of fact, a blade is tossed to

26

and fro by every wind of doctrine. People jump from church to church; they have one spiritual father this week, but a new spiritual father next week. This is how a leader knows when your gift is still at blade level. You have to be careful with blades because they cut people. When you haven't gained mastery over your gifts, you'll cut people while you're prophesying to them. They would be worse off when you left then than they were before they encountered you.

There's first the blade, and then, the ear. The second stage of emergence is the stage of coaching. First, you have cultivation. Next, there's coaching. Why? Because someone has to teach you how to move with the wind. After the blade, the ear emerges. How well is your hearing? Gifts have to be coachable. For example, if I was an actor and I was told to do a monologue, I could start the monologue screaming, "Where were you?!" My director would stop me and say that I'm spending too much energy at the beginning. He would say, "You're about to get into a fight, but the fight is going to build up, and I want it to take time to build up because you're really not mad at what she did, you're mad about the last ten years. So, don't spend all of your energy in one moment. Don't come out screaming, 'Where were you?' Just ask the question in a calm tone." He would tell me to hold back some of the energy and the tension. What the director would be doing is seeing how coachable I am. This is a multidimensional test that's not just used in the world of theater, it's also used in the world of preaching. Your pastor could say, "You went ten minutes over your time teaching your message, so this time, I'm going to only give you five minutes." Your pastor is not constricting you, your pastor is coaching you. A blade sees coaching or correction as constriction, but an ear understands the difference.

After the ear, then arises the full corn in the ear. Even when corn has matured, it is still covered! My brothers and I used to shuck corn. I'm not talking about the corn you get from Kroger, I'm talking about the corn that still has the worms inside of it. Now, when you get a piece of corn, you cannot see its gifting. When you get a piece of corn, you cannot see what we call its meat because it is covered. Even when it's mature, it's still covered. Nobody knows what's in there unless they start peeling back the layers. Every gift should be covered in layers. That's the corn's mantle. These are stages of emergence.

Genesis 37:5-6 reads, "And Joseph dreamed a dream, and he told it his brethren: and they hated him yet the more. And he said unto them, Hear, I pray you, this dream which I have dreamed: For, behold, we were binding sheaves in the field, and, lo, my sheaf arose ..." Now, when he's talking about sheaf, he's talking about wheat. Before he ever looked up into the sky, he was dealing with the earth below. What Joseph was being initiated into is the promise of Abraham. God told Abraham to go outside and look at the sand of the seashore. He told him that's how his offspring would be. He told Abraham to look at the stars in the heavens; that was how his offspring would be. So, when Joseph was having a dream, he was dreaming in both dimensions; he had a dream about what would happen on Earth and he dreamed about what would happen in Heaven. What I'm trying to get you to understand is that the dream was about the same thing. We're dealing with the Earth right now, but we have to get to the heavens, so the same way a star is formed is the same way a piece of vegetation is formed; it begins underneath the surface. When I say star, I'm talking about a gifted person. When God wants to rearrange or redistribute influence or authority, He causes a new gift to emerge. One gift emerging changes the economy of a region.

Genesis 1:3 reads, "And God said, Let there be light: and there was light." Now, of course, we're going to come to understand that God created the sun, moon and the stars on the fourth day. The theological question is, if God didn't create the light beings until the fourth day, what was this particular light that Genesis 1:3 references? The scriptures tell us that God is Light. The word "light" in the Hebrew text is not just a word, it's a concept. I want to give you a few words that define or denote the concept of light.

1. **Knowledge:** In the scriptures, whenever you see light, it's also referencing knowledge. Adversely, the lack of light means the lack of knowledge. God said, "My people perish for the lack of knowledge." The Bible also talks about sinners sitting in gross darkness. That's a lack of knowledge, and of course, knowledge that is not human is also divine. This brings us to our second bullet point.
2. **Revelation:** Light represents revelation. When we talk about revelation, we're talking about revealed knowledge. This is something that your human intellect could not grasp; this is something that had to be revealed by God.
3. **Wisdom:** In the absence of light, you wouldn't know what to do. Wisdom is the light that radiates from within. Ecclesiastes 8:1 says, "Who is as the wise man? And who knoweth the interpretation of a thing? A man's wisdom maketh his face to shine, and the boldness of his face shall be changed."
4. **Exposure:** Don't think about this word using sin consciousness because people become weird when we use the word "expose." This is because the average person is hiding something. When we talk about exposure, we're not just talking about hiding stuff, but there are things that you cannot find without light. In Luke 15, a woman lost a coin in her house. In other words, when there is a lack of light, there is an inability to discern value. That's why people fornicate in the dark.
5. **Glory:** Revelation 21:23 says it this way, "And the city had no need of the sun, neither of the moon, to shine in it: for the glory of God did lighten it, and the Lamb *is* the light thereof."

In Genesis 1:14, God said, "Let there be light in the firmaments." The word "firmament" means space. On the first day, God said, "Let there be light." Hear me—light without space creates a shadow. Light needs space to function because light must travel 386,000 miles per second. So, God said, "Let there be light." Since there was no space, there was nothing but pressure and heat. Consequently, God had to say, "Let there be space." That word "firmament" means space. It means room. God literally said, "Let there be room" and space was literally created. Once space was created, light began to travel because information needs a platform, revelation needs a platform and wisdom needs a platform. If you have good advice, your advice is worthless if people don't give you a platform to share it on. When I say space, I'm talking about a platform. Wisdom and knowledge mean nothing without a platform. I want you to understand that when I say space, I'm talking about a platform. Let's say, for example, that I was talking about a stage—let there be lights in the firmaments, let there be lights in the space or let there be lights on the stage.

Genesis 37 talks about Joseph's dream. It reads, "And he dreamed yet another dream, and told it his brethren, and said, Behold, I have dreamed a dream more; and, behold, the sun and the moon and the eleven stars made obeisance to me. And he told it to his father, and to his brethren: and his father rebuked him, and said unto him, What is this dream that thou hast dreamed? Shall I and thy mother and thy brethren indeed come to bow down ourselves to thee to the earth?" Get this—Joseph's father interpreted the dream! He said, "Will I, your mother and your brothers bow down to you?" The sun represents the father, the mother is represented by the moon, and the brothers are represented by stars. If we were to interpret this biblically, the sun is Father God; He is the Source (Abba, Father) of all light, all wisdom, all revelation, all knowledge, and all power. This is also because He is the center of our solar system and because the sun represents light. He is the focus of all of our movements. The moon represents the church; the moon does not create her own light.

Instead, the church reflects the light from the Father. It is the moon that gives off light during the night. Jesus said, "I must work the works of the One who sent me while it is day for night comes where no man can work." The night deals with

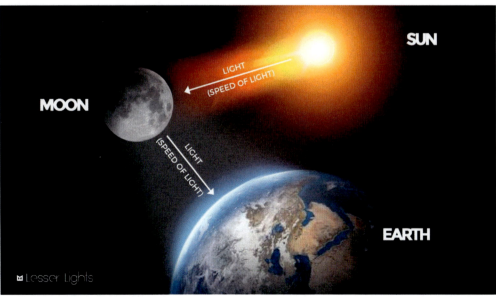

the darkest of hours—demonic times. And it is the job of the church to shine bright in the darkest of times. That's what the moon is there for—to reflect the light. The moon goes through stages—full moon, half moon, quarter moon and no moon. Every stage of the moon represents the maturity of the church, which goes through cycles.

Every generation of the church has to mature, so it starts off a crescent moon, a quarter moon, a gibbous moon and then a full moon. Based on its positioning, it will reveal certain levels of light. The church can only reflect as much light as it is in the right position. This is why Matthew 6:33 is important. "But seek ye first the kingdom of God, and his righteousness; and all these things shall be added unto you." Righteousness doesn't mean you doing good stuff, it means that you are in the right position. You don't have to be good to reflect the light of God, you just need to be in the right position. The stars represent the brethren—we are the stars. The stars represent the saints in the congregation. Each one of them emit a certain level of light and radiance, but together, they can lighten a dark sky. When stars come together, they are called constellations.

Let's briefly deal with zodiac signs. Because the curse that many people are dealing with is in their constellation. Every star has a constellation; it's their circle. It's called their relationships or their friendships. This is why zodiac signs were never from God. For example, have you ever read your horoscope, and you were amazed at how accurate it appeared to be? Get this—zodiac signs allow you to get revelation of who you are without God. It locks or compartmentalizes you into this theme, and you start to feel like that's who you are supposed to be. Consequently, you start saying things like, "I'm a Taurus; that's why I got anger issues!" And as long as you identify yourself as a Taurus, you will have anger issues! Remember, you are born again; your life is hidden in Christ in God! There is no longer Jew nor Greek, Capricorn or Sagittarius! You see, the stars don't have the ability to change you, but the Holy Ghost has the ability to change you! God don't want you getting your personality from stars! Read that again! God doesn't want you getting your personality from stars (celebrities)! "You are wearied with your many counsels; let them stand forth and save you, those who divide the heavens, who gaze at the stars, who at the new moons make known what shall come upon you. Behold, they are like stubble; the fire consumes them; they cannot deliver themselves from the power of the flame." (Isaiah 47:13-14).

Prophetic Activation

Today, call someone who you haven't spoken with in a long time (at least six months). Tell that person that you love him or her and just encourage the individual. Also, if God gives you something, prophesy over that person's life. Don't be shy! If you go to voicemail, leave the individual a message and call him or her back until you get him or her on the phone!

Mission Three

T-07

5-18-20

<u>Just Talking</u>

<u>Relaunch</u>

<u>Shifting</u>

<u>Rod fishing — scratching</u>

CLARITY
God putting a demand
Pressure

Checking setting clarity
bridge pioneer

A bridge of the world + church
talk worldly to express spirituality
get clarity of purpose
    How are you growing the local assembly
Use the talent
Priest + King under order of Melchisedek
(all)

Clarity in reading chapter tonight
— Confessional —
— new Limp new Name

[VISION MISSION]
[Brand — marketing]

— Teacher — being educated
— Jest — Joker don't make joke

Ministry + Lifestyle
You have had time to prepared — We hitting the ground running

Spectrum — teaching — Standard
        — measurement
        — Master the language of the house —

Prophetic Functions

First and foremost, let's establish (for some) or reestablish (for others) what a prophet is. The Greek word for "prophet" is "prophétés" and it literally means a forth-teller or an interpreter. The following was taken from Help Word Studies:

> **Cognate: 4396:** *prophḗtēs* (from 4253 /*pró*, "beforehand" and 5346 /*phēmí*, "elevating/asserting one idea over another, especially through the spoken-word") – properly, one who *speaks forth* by the inspiration of God; a *prophet*.
> A prophet declares the mind (message) of God, which sometimes predicts the future (foretelling) – and more commonly, *speaks forth.* His message for a particular situation. 4396 /*prophḗtēs* ("a prophet") then is someone inspired by God to *foretell* or *tell-forth* (*forthtell*) the Word of God.

In short, a prophet is a man or woman who expresses what's on the heart and mind of God; someone who has been elected by God to stand in as a medium between Himself and mankind. This means that every believer who is prophetic is not a prophet. A prophet is preordained by God to be His mouthpiece, whereas, a prophetic individual is someone who has the Holy Spirit and can readily hear from Him. But before we go any further, let's address this word "medium," since it is now being used in the occult world, and because of this, the church at large is trying to distance themselves from this word. The word "medium" means a go-between. The Greek word for "medium" is "mesos" and it means middle, between or in the midst of. The reason I'm sharing this is so that we, as the church, should not be intimidated by this word or any other word in the English language. A prophet is a medium; he or she is the go-between or the connector between God and man. A witch is a medium; he or she is a go-between or the connector between Satan and man. And while, as the church, we don't use the word "medium" when referencing prophets, we do need to understand that a prophet of God is the middle-ground or meeting place between God and His people.

What is the function of a prophet? Jeremiah 1:10 answers this question; it reads, "See, I have this day set thee over the nations and over the kingdoms, to root out, and to pull down, and to destroy, and to throw down, to build, and to plant." So, the function of a prophet is to:

1. To root out
2. To pull down
3. To destroy
4. To throw down
5. To build
6. To plant

In *Prophetic Science, Session One*, we established the functions of a prophet, but in this section, we'll go more in detail. This will help us to understand the lifestyles that we commonly see amongst God's mouthpieces.

Function One: To Root Out

Matthew 13:24-28: Another parable put he forth unto them, saying, The kingdom of heaven is likened unto a man which sowed good seed in his field: But while men slept, his enemy came and sowed tares among the wheat, and went his way. But when the blade was sprung up, and brought forth fruit, then appeared the tares also. So the servants of the householder came and said unto him, Sir, didst not thou sow good seed in thy field? From whence then hath it tares? He said unto them, An enemy hath done this.

Matthew 13:37-43: He answered and said unto them, He that soweth the good seed is the Son of man; the field is the world; the good seed are the children of the kingdom; but the tares are the children of the wicked one; The enemy that sowed them is the devil; the harvest is the end of the world; and the reapers are the angels. As therefore the tares are gathered and burned in the fire; so shall it be in the end of this world. The Son of man shall send forth his angels, and they shall gather out of his kingdom all things that offend, and them which do iniquity; and shall cast them into a furnace of fire: there shall be wailing and gnashing of teeth. Then shall the righteous shine forth as the sun in the kingdom of their Father. Who hath ears to hear, let him hear.

Wheat has an evil twin that the Bible refers to as "tares." Tares are believed to be what we now call "darnels," which is a type of ryegrass. Here are a few facts about darnels:
1. They look just like wheat in their youth, but are considered weeds.
2. They look remarkably like wheat until the ear appears. The ears of the darnel plant become black once they mature, whereas, the ears of wheat remain brown.
3. Darnels are referred to as "false wheat" in some regions.
4. Consumption of this plant causes the person to experience drunken nausea.
5. The poison in this plant can be fatal.

Most people, including farmers, cannot tell the difference between tares and wheat until the ears appear. But notice here that the servants mentioned in the parable were able to discern the plant almost immediately. They were able to discern between the wheat and the tares before the ears began to form! This means that the servants were mature, discerning, and most of all, they loved their master! Hear me—most folks in the church love to talk about false shepherds, false prophets and false teachers, and while that's all well and good, no one is talking about false wheat! This is why we have so many pastors quitting every year; this is why we have so many pastors taking their own lives or losing their minds! One of the duties of a prophet is to sniff these people out! Another word for this is discernment! As a prophet or a prophetic type, your job isn't to confront tares, the scriptures say to "mark them that sow discord among you!" The Bible also tells us to watch and pray! Lastly, a prophet's job isn't to gossip about the tares, a prophet's job is to warn the leaders of an organization, and then, proceed to pray!

Every organization has its own culture, sound and DNA. The job or role of the leaders of each organization is to not only establish a culture, but to sustain it. The job of false wheat is to pervert the culture of an organization. You see, if you change the sound, the culture, the DNA or the fingerprint of an organization, you effectively unseat the authority of that place! The official term for this is "usurping authority."

Consider the Garden of Eden. It was a beautiful place, filled with life and greenery. In the midst of the Garden stood a tree called the Tree of the Knowledge of Good and Evil. God told Adam and Eve to not touch this tree. Even though the fruit on the tree was ripe and ready for consumption, it was still forbidden; even though the tree was in the Garden, it was still forbidden. The couple disobeyed God, and as a result, they were poisoned by their own ambitions, they were poisoned by their own lusts, they were poisoned by their own discontentment! Consequently, death attached itself to the atoms of mankind through Adam and Eve; it twisted our DNA and the first generational curse that we'd ever wrestle with was born. The million-dollar question is, who planted the Tree of the Knowledge of Good and Evil in the Garden of Eden, and was the tree itself evil? The tree, within itself, wasn't evil. Each tree in the Garden represented the mind of God. Every time Adam and Eve ate from one of the trees in the Garden, they were literally taking in the knowledge of God, meaning, even though they were perfect, they didn't know everything. They were still growing in their knowledge; they were still growing in their intimacy with God! God wanted them to pursue Him by pursuing knowledge. This is why He would often meet with Adam in the cool of the day. He was measuring the wheat! He was seeing how much Adam had grown! And even though every tree represented the mind of God, there was some knowledge that God didn't want the couple to have. He didn't want them to familiarize themselves with the world of sin. Think about some of the mafia's original kingpins. They were killing people and running multi-million-dollar criminal organizations, but they kept their wives in the dark about their "professions." They showered them with money, gifts and gave them lavish lifestyles, but they put as much distance between their wives and their criminal activities as they possibly could. They did this because they didn't want their wives to deal with the weight of their choices. The women couldn't be charged or convicted for whatever they did not know! So, if drugs were found in their homes, if weapons were found in their homes or if bodies were found in their homes, the wives would be found

Prophetic Functions

innocent simply because they were ignorant of their husbands' lifestyles. And while we know that the mafia is a dark organization, it does give us some insight into God's reasoning. What they didn't know truly could not hurt them!

To obey God is sacrifice; to disobey Him is sin. This means that the sin was not found in the fruit of the tree, it was found in the couple's disobedience. To intentionally or knowingly sin against God is called rebellion, and the Bible tells us that rebellion is like the sin of witchcraft! Eve hadn't been poisoned by the fruit; she'd been poisoned by the lies. Let's review the story. "Now the serpent was more subtil than any beast of the field which the LORD God had made. And he said unto the woman, Yea, hath God said, Ye shall not eat of every tree of the garden? And the woman said unto the serpent, We may eat of the fruit of the trees of the garden: But of the fruit of the tree which is in the midst of the garden, God hath said, Ye shall not eat of it, neither shall ye touch it, lest ye die. And the serpent said unto the woman, Ye shall not surely die: For God doth know that in the day ye eat thereof, then your eyes shall be opened, and ye shall be as gods, knowing good and evil" (Genesis 3:1-5).

The Tree of the Knowledge of Good and Evil gives us a picture of what a sinner looks like in the midst of believers. They are attractive, they are enticing and they can be both poisonous and venomous.

Word	Definition	Word	Definition
Poison	a substance that through its chemical action usually kills, injures, or impairs an organism.	**Venom**	a toxic substance produced by some animals (such as snakes, scorpions, or bees) that is injected into prey or an enemy chiefly by biting or stinging and has an injurious or lethal effect.
Poisonous	producing a toxic substance that causes injury or death when absorbed or ingested.	**Venomous**	producing venom in a specialized gland and capable of inflicting injury or death.

(Definitions taken from Merriam Webster's Online Dictionary)

In short, poisons are often ingested or absorbed, whereas, venom is injected through an attack. Make no mistake about it, the couple was attacked in the Garden of Eden, but Satan didn't attack them directly. He attacked their theology; he attacked their relationship with God, but he could not do this without their will. So, he planted some lies in the midst of the truth. He then tempted Eve with the lies. In other words, Eve had been poisoned. She willfully bit into the lie, but eating from the tree was just the fruit of her belief system. You see, when Satan lied to her, Eve's sin was believing him over God. This was the root of her sin, but her choice to disobey God was the fruit of her sin. She then took that fruit to Adam and poisoned him as well. After that, the couple became venomous, meaning, their children would be born full of the very toxins that the couple had taken in; their children would have sin attached to their DNA. But this didn't automatically mean they'd all choose darkness over light. Cain chose to be evil, but Abel chose to worship God. Both men grew up together in the same home, but instead of poisoning Abel, Cain attacked and killed him. This was his venomous nature manifesting itself.

Sons and daughters were born to Adam and Eve and to their children. Slowly, but surely, the Earth began to be filled with evil men along with men who truly desired to serve YAHWEH. God's desire was and is to bring everyone to the saving knowledge of His Word, so He sent forth prophets and prophetic types to serve as lights in the darkness. Your assignment is to destroy the works of the devil, and one of the ways that you do this is through discernment.

Function Two: To Pull Down

Be sure to open your companion Bible and read the story of Elijah's confrontation with Ahab and the people of Israel. This story details one of the most epic biblical showdowns to date. To read the story in its entirety, turn to 1 Kings. I've listed the end of the story below.

1 Kings 18:36-40: And it came to pass at the time of the offering of the evening sacrifice, that Elijah the prophet came near, and said, LORD God of Abraham, Isaac, and of Israel, let it be known this day that thou art God in Israel, and that I am thy servant, and that I have done all these things at thy word. Hear me, O LORD, hear me, that this people may know that thou art the LORD God, and that thou hast turned their heart back again. Then the fire of the LORD fell, and consumed the burnt sacrifice, and the wood, and the stones, and the dust, and licked up the water that was in the trench. And when all the people saw it, they fell on their faces: and they said, The LORD, he is the God; the LORD, he is the God. And Elijah said unto them, Take the prophets of Baal; let not one of them escape. And they took them: and Elijah brought them down to the brook Kishon, and slew them there.

After the tares have been identified, the next assignment of a prophet or prophetic type is to pull down "high things." What are "high things?"

| Formula | Philosophy | Stronghold | Culture | Tradition | Principle | Statute |

High Thing	Definition (Merriam Webster)
Philosophy	a search for a general understanding of values and reality by chiefly speculative rather than observational means.
Stronghold	a place dominated by a particular group or marked by a particular characteristic.
Culture	the customary beliefs, social forms, and material traits of a racial, religious, or social group.
Tradition	an inherited, established, or customary pattern of thought, action, or behavior (such as a religious practice or a social custom).
Principle	a comprehensive and fundamental law, doctrine, or assumption.
Statute	a law enacted by the legislative branch of a government.

Prophets pull down statutes, ungodly cultures, traditions, philosophies, principles and strongholds; all of these "high things" set the tone for idolatry. An idol is the fruit of a person or a group's belief system, and this is why prophets are called to confront idols by confronting the beliefs, lies and doctrines that are present in certain regions, families, tribes and organizations. Think of it this way—you're walking through a garden filled with wheat and tares. Your discernment kicks in! You see the tares and decide to uproot them, but there's a problem—the people who eat from the garden strongly believe that the tares are wheat. Some of the people who've eaten from that garden have gotten sick or worse, however, it's difficult, if not impossible, to convince the people to allow you to root out the tares. As a matter of fact, the law says that without the permission of the people, you can't do anything, so your job is to convince the people at large that there are tares amongst them. But you don't do this by having an emotional shouting match or by humiliating the tares; you do this by teaching the truth, in love. You also do this through prayer and fasting. This means that a true, mature prophet of God must be patient and knowledgeable! Hear me—prophets cannot be easily offended, impatient or ignorant! Moses said to Pharaoh, "Thus saith the LORD God of Israel, Let my people go, that they may hold a feast unto me in the wilderness." This sounds simple enough, but the scriptures tell us that God hardened Pharaoh's heart! This was so that He could build the faith of the people! But can you imagine if Moses had been like many of the 21st century prophets?! What if he was impatient? What if he had been anxious to prove to all of Israel just how powerful he was?! How thin would our Bibles be if the prophets and patriarchs of old had been impatient, ambitious, prideful or rebellious? Lastly, think about the Tree of the Knowledge of Good and Evil. What if it had been an evil tree planted in the midst of the Garden by Satan, himself? How would Adam and Eve pull it down? It's simple—they wouldn't cut it down, they'd simply refuse to eat from it, touch it or water it! Get this—a false prophet is ineffective if he or she has no followers! This is why you never go after the false prophet, you go after the sheep! False prophets are known to go after other false prophets in an attempt to legitimize their own platforms, but true and mature prophets go after the sheep! In Matthew 18:12, Jesus said, "How think ye? If a man have an hundred sheep, and one of them be gone astray, doth he not leave the ninety and nine, and goeth into the mountains, and seeketh that which is gone astray?" True prophets are not wolf-centered; they are sheep-centered! Of course, this doesn't mean that you have to ignore the wolves—the Bible says to mark them that cause division among you, and we all know that wolves like to divide and conquer! But if you change the mind of the sheep, you render the wolf powerless!

What Elijah did was get the people to change their minds; he got them to repent of their idolatry, and he reestablished the worship of God in Israel. But his job wasn't done just yet! You see, changing the mind of the people is a temporary fix if you don't destroy the demonic system or confront the strongman! This brings us to function three!

Function Three: To Destroy

1 Kings 18:40: And Elijah said unto them, Take the prophets of Baal; let not one of them escape. And they took them: and Elijah brought them down to the brook Kishon, and slew them there.

After Elijah proved once and for all that YAHWEH is the only true and living God, he had to confront the system of Baal worship. To do this, he had to bind and destroy the operators behind that system. But he couldn't do this on his own. He'd gotten the people to repent, but it was now time for them to confront their own demons; they had to arrest and slaughter the prophets of Baal. These prophets represented the system of Baal. Without them, the practice of Baal worship could not be sustained.

Prophets confront, dismantle and destroy systems by first proving that YAHWEH is the only true and living God. The prophet's assignment is to turn the hearts of the people back to God before destroying the demonic systems (altars) that were put in place as a result of those beliefs and the demonic workers behind those altars. Please understand that systems and strongholds are not one in the same. A stronghold, according to Merriam Webster is:
- a fortified place
- a place of security or survival

Strongholds have to be pulled down; these are the philosophies and beliefs that we discussed under function two. In short, a stronghold can be and oftentimes is what we refer to as a "comfort zone." These are largely guarded beliefs that we defend so rigorously. The stronghold was the Israelites believing that Baal was their god, the system involved the altars and the priests that worked behind those altars, and the strongman, in this case, was Jezebel.

A system is "a regularly interacting or interdependent group of items forming a unified whole" (Source: Merriam Webster). A system, in layman's terms, is a body with many members, all of which work together for a single purpose. Systems require energy to work. The human body is a system, the governmental body is a system, marriage is a system, the church is a system—all of these are bodies. Every body has members, and all of the members function in one of the bodies many systems, for example:
- The legs and arms are members of the human body.
- The United States government has many branches, and each branch has members, for example, the U.S. Senate has members.
- The husband and wife are both members in a marital unit.
- We are all members of the body of Christ.
- We are all members of a church.

Again, a system is a body with many members, all of which work together for a single purpose. What is the purpose of a demonic system? The simple answer is—to usurp God's authority and to overthrow the government of the Kingdom of God. Believe it or not, Satan still covets God's seat of authority; this isn't a secret. But what could he possibly do to accomplish his goals? When an authority figure wanted to remove or replace another authority figure in the biblical days, he would attack one system by destroying another. He would do this through violence or by turning the hearts of the people. Satan and his angels had already waged war in Heaven and lost, so the next method of warfare they used was to turn the hearts of man away from God. What does this look like? It looked like Satan walking up to Eve in the Garden of Eden and gossiping about God. What he'd done was got her to exchange the system of honor for a system of dishonor. To finalize the change, he had to get her to invest in her beliefs. She had to make a sacrifice. Eve made three sacrifices on that day:
- She sacrificed her relationship with God.
- She sacrificed herself.
- She poisoned her husband.

In order to overturn a system, a new one has to be put in place; a new sacrifice has to be made. This is why Jesus came into the Earth. "He that committeth sin is of the devil; for the devil sinneth from the beginning. For this purpose the Son of God was manifested, that he might destroy the works of the devil" (1 John 3:8).

It also It looked like Absalom turning the hearts of the Israelites to himself so that he could dethrone his father. Let's review his story. " And Absalom rose up early, and stood beside the way of the gate: and it was so, that when any man that had a controversy came to the king for judgment, then Absalom called unto him, and said, Of what city art thou? And he said, Thy servant is of one of the tribes of Israel. And Absalom said unto him, See, thy matters are good and right; but there is no man deputed of the king to hear thee. Absalom said moreover, Oh that I were made judge in the land, that every man which hath any suit or cause might come unto me, and I would do him justice! And it was so, that when any man came nigh to him to do him obeisance, he put forth his hand, and took him, and kissed him. And on this manner did Absalom to all Israel that came to the king for judgment: so Absalom stole the hearts of the men of Israel." (2 Kings 15:2-6).

Absalom, like most tares or false wheat, was incredibly patient. He slowly turned the hearts of the Jews in his direction before he decided to wage war against his father. He was going against the system that had been in place—this system is what we call the system of honor. A system, in short, is nothing but a compilation of philosophies and principles, all of which work together to secure a structure. When these beliefs settle, they become strongholds. Another word for stronghold is "habit."
- It takes, on average, 66 days to form a habit.
- It takes, on average, 21 days to break a habit.

Habits that are established and exercised over a period of time often become cultures. When a culture is passed down from one generation to the next, it becomes a tradition. Of course, when religion or the government gets involved, a culture or a tradition can easily become a statute. Look at the chart below to get a better understanding.

Levels	High Thing	Ascension
First	Philosophy	Individual, Familial Belief System
Second	Stronghold	Corporate Belief System
Third	Culture	Communal Belief System (Cult, Occult)
Fourth	Tradition	Generational Belief System
Fifth	Principle	Religious Belief System (Doctrine)
Sixth	Statue	Governmental Belief System (Law)

Prophets destroy these systems by confronting the ideologies and theologies that they are built on. This is how false prophets and false teachers are dethroned. Any person who tries to confront an organizational head without first dismantling a demonic system opens the door for demonic reentry. Prophets deal with the roots of systems, while Apostles deal with the heads of systems. The roots represent the origin or the foundation, whereas, the head represents the authority. A prophet's job is to completely obliterate the system until there is no trace of it to be found. But to do this, the prophet must first confront the beliefs of the people, get the people to repent, and then, once their hearts are turned back to God, the prophet gets the people to destroy the old systems that had been put in place as a result of those beliefs. The Israelites had to destroy the worship of Baal and reestablish the worship of YAHWEH. Prophet Elijah confronted the people, and then, he got them to confront and kill the false prophets. What he was doing was dismantling a demonic system. This was the legality. Remember this rule, you must first confront a legality before you attempt to overthrow a principality.

Function Four: To Throw Down

2 Kings 9:1-3: And Elisha the prophet called one of the children of the prophets, and said unto him, Gird up thy loins, and take this box of oil in thine hand, and go to Ramothgilead: And when thou comest thither, look out there Jehu the son of Jehoshaphat the son of Nimshi, and go in, and make him arise up from among his brethren, and carry him to an inner chamber; then take the box of oil, and pour it on his head, and say, Thus saith the LORD, I have anointed thee king over Israel. Then open the door, and flee, and tarry not.

2 Kings 9:24-29: And Jehu drew a bow with his full strength, and smote Jehoram between his arms, and the arrow went out at his heart, and he sunk down in his chariot. Then said Jehu to Bidkar his captain, Take up, and cast him in the portion of the field of Naboth the Jezreelite: for remember how that, when I and thou rode together after Ahab his father, the LORD laid this burden upon him; surely I have seen yesterday the blood of Naboth, and the blood of his sons, saith the LORD; and I will requite thee in this plat, saith the LORD. Now therefore take and cast him into the plat of ground, according to the word of the LORD. But when Ahaziah the king of Judah saw this, he fled by the way of the garden house. And Jehu followed after him, and said, Smite him also in the chariot. And they did so at the going up to Gur, which is by Ibleam. And he fled to Megiddo, and died there. And his servants carried him in a chariot to Jerusalem, and buried him in his sepulchre with his fathers in the city of David. And in the eleventh year of Joram the son of Ahab began Ahaziah to reign over Judah.

2 Kings 9:30-33: And when Jehu was come to Jezreel, Jezebel heard of it; and she painted her face, and tired her head, and looked out at a window. And as Jehu entered in at the gate, she said, Had Zimri peace, who slew his master? And he lifted up his face to the window, and said, Who is on my side? Who? And there looked out to him two or three eunuchs. And he said, Throw her down. So they threw her down: and some of her blood was sprinkled on the wall, and on the horses: and he trode her under foot.

2 Kings 10:25-28: And it came to pass, as soon as he had made an end of offering the burnt offering, that Jehu said to the guard and to the captains, Go in, and slay them; let none come forth. And they smote them with the edge of the sword; and the guard and the captains cast them out, and went to the city of the house of Baal. And they brought forth the images out of the house of Baal, and burned them. And they brake down the image of Baal, and brake down the house of Baal, and made it a draught house unto this day. **Thus Jehu destroyed Baal out of Israel.**

Once the system had been destroyed, the statute or the law could be destroyed. A law is a legality. Another word for "throw down" is to overthrow. As you can see in the aforementioned scriptures, Jehu systematically began to overthrow the authorities that had been set in place—these were the authorities who'd supported and sustained the worship of Baal. This is a principle of deliverance—after dealing with the systems and binding the henchmen, you have to cast out the strongman, otherwise, he'll return. After the stronghold had been broken, after the demonic systems had been dismantled, the strongman had to be overthrown. When the men and women confessed that YAHWEH is God and they killed the prophets of Baal, they'd gone through their first round of deliverance. The next round of deliverance would involve Jehu, but before Jehu could confront Jezebel, he had to be anointed as king of Israel. This is another principle of deliverance. You have to outrank a spirit in order to overthrow it. If you come across a spirit that you cannot cast out, it could simply mean that there is a legality in place that has not been dismantled or it could mean that you haven't been anointed to confront the strongman. Apostle Paul said it this way, "I have planted, Apollos watered; but God gave the increase" (1 Corinthians 3:6). In other words, you can't do this alone. This was the mistake that Elijah made. He'd convinced himself that he was the only prophet left, and because of this, the journey became too much for him to bear. Consequently, God had to raise someone else up in his stead. He raised up Elisha who eventually anointed Jehu.

Jezebel had been a star, but the time had come for her to become a fallen star. According to science, to kill a star, you have to swap out the hydrogen in the star with iron. This means that you have to remove what's fueling the star. What fueled Jezebel was the support she'd received from the Israelites. The source of her authority had been Ahab, but he had already been killed in the war between Israel and Ramoth-Gilead. Once Elijah had successfully turned the hearts of the people back to YAHWEH, Jezebel began to run out of fuel. When a star runs out of fuel, it begins to collapse under its own weight. Jezebel was tossed out of her high place; she was removed from her seat of authority and Israel was purged from her witchcraft.

Ahab's legacy was destroyed to keep his idolatrous and murderous bloodline from spreading. He had seventy sons, but because of his wickedness, God sent Jehu after all of them. They were assassinated for two reasons:
1. God wanted to purge Israel of Jezebel's witchcraft. To do this, He had to dethrone Jezebel and kill off the prophets of Baal.
2. Her sons had a claim to the throne, so if Jezebel and Ahab were murdered, one of their sons would have risen in their places and continued to promote the worship of Baal.

You'll notice that God told Jehu to "smite" the house of Ahab. Other translations use the word "destroy." He said that He would cut off everyone who "pisseth against a wall," meaning, every male in Ahab's lineage was to be killed. What God was dealing with was the system of Baal worship that had become a statute in all of Israel. To pull down this legality and to override this demonic system, God had to send a clear message to His people—He was and is the only True and Living God. To send a message (prophecy), He had to send a messenger (prophet). So, He had Jehu anointed as king over Israel, but in that time, prophets would anoint the kings and queens. They themselves couldn't lay a finger on a king, nor could they legally lay a finger on a queen, so to dethrone a wicked ruler, they had to anoint another ruler in their place. Prophets could slaughter false prophets; this is why Elijah commanded that the prophets of Baal be killed, but they could not order the assassination of a king or a queen. A king, on the other hand, could overthrow another king or queen. Today, we use the word "cast out," when overthrowing a strongman.

Function Five: To Build

In Exodus 27:1-19, God gave Moses instructions to build a temple for Him. Be sure to read those instructions in your companion Bible. Throughout the scriptures, you'll notice that anytime God destroyed a system, He established a new one. When the Israelites would fall into the clutches, the snares and the ditches of idolatry, God would raise up a king, a patriarch or a prophet to dismantle the strongholds, dethrone the strongmen and reestablish His name amongst the people. Some of the chosen ones destroyed demonic systems in their entirety, while others partially dealt with them.

High places represented philosophies, strongholds, principles, statutes, cultures and traditions, however, the altars and the priests or prophets that stood on those high places represented systems. If you destroyed the altar but not the system, it would be only a matter of time before the people returned to idolatry. If you destroyed the high place, you would overturn the system, but someone would rise up and rebuild it. So, a prophet had to obliterate pagan altars and utterly destroy the high places. This was important, but what was just as important was replacing the old system with a new one. Prophets would tear down the pagan altars and erect altars for YAHWEH. If a new altar was not built, the people would return to what they knew—idolatry. So, a prophet's job is not complete until he or she has initiated a new system. The patriarchs wouldn't just tear down demonic altars, they would erect new altars. Altars represent systems; they marked the end of an era or a season, and the beginning of a new era or season. This is the law of replacement. This law dictates that God doesn't remove a thing without first replacing it. Consider Matthew 12:43-45, which states, "When the unclean spirit is gone out of a man, he walketh through dry places, seeking rest, and findeth none. Then he saith, I will return into my house from whence I came out; and when he is come, he findeth it empty, swept, and garnished. Then goeth he, and taketh with himself seven other spirits more wicked than himself, and they enter in and dwell there: and the last state of that man is worse than the first. Even so shall it be also unto this wicked generation."

One of the mistakes that Jehu made was that he did not restore the worship of God; he did not build an altar to God, and this, of course, was because he had not established an altar in his personal life with God. 2 Kings 10:29-31 reads, "Howbeit from the sins of Jeroboam the son of Nebat, who made Israel to sin, Jehu departed not from after them, to wit, the golden calves that were in Bethel, and that were in Dan. And the LORD said unto Jehu, Because thou hast done well in executing that which is right in mine eyes, and hast done unto the house of Ahab according to all that was in mine heart, thy children of the fourth generation shall sit on the throne of Israel. But Jehu took no heed to walk in the law of the LORD God of Israel with all his heart: for he departed not from the sins of Jeroboam, which made Israel to sin."

Anytime a prophet does not personally devote time to God, that prophet will inevitably fall into the same pit that he or she was assigned to throw God's enemies into. Anytime an altar is destroyed, a new altar or a new system has to be erected in its place. Because Jehu did not establish or build any altars for God, Athaliah (Jezebel's daughter) rose up and became queen over Judah. 2 Kings 11:3 reads, "And when Athaliah the mother of Ahaziah saw that her son was dead, she arose and destroyed all the seed royal. But Jehosheba, the daughter of king Joram, sister of Ahaziah, took Joash the son of Ahaziah, and stole him from among the king's sons which were slain; and they hid him, even him and his nurse, in the bedchamber from Athaliah, so that he was not slain. And he was with her hid in the house of the LORD six years. And Athaliah did reign over the land."

Kings/Rulers over Israel

King/Ruler	High Place/ System Destroyed?	Scripture
Jehoahaz Evil	No	**2 Kings 13:1-2:** In the three and twentieth year of Joash the son of Ahaziah king of Judah Jehoahaz the son of Jehu began to reign over Israel in Samaria, and reigned seventeen years. And he did that which was evil in the sight of the LORD, and followed the sins of Jeroboam the son of Nebat, which made Israel to sin; he departed not therefrom.
Jehoash Evil	No	**2 Kings 13:10-11:** In the thirty and seventh year of Joash king of Judah began Jehoash the son of Jehoahaz to reign over Israel in Samaria, and reigned sixteen years. And he did that which was evil in the sight of the LORD; he departed not from all the sins of Jeroboam the son of Nebat, who made Israel sin: but he walked therein.
Jeroboam II Evil	No	**2 Kings 14:23-24:** In the fifteenth year of Amaziah the son of Joash king of Judah Jeroboam the son of Joash king of Israel began to reign in Samaria, and reigned forty and one years. And he did that which was evil in the sight of the LORD: he departed not from all the sins of Jeroboam the son of Nebat, who made Israel to sin.
Zachariah Evil	No	**2 Kings 15:8-9:** In the thirty and eighth year of Azariah king of Judah did Zachariah the son of Jeroboam reign over Israel in Samaria six months. And he did that which was evil in the sight of the LORD, as his fathers had done: he departed not from the sins of Jeroboam the son of Nebat, who made Israel to sin.
Shallum N/A	No	**2 Kings 15:13-15:** Shallum the son of Jabesh began to reign in the nine and thirtieth year of Uzziah king of Judah; and he reigned a full month in Samaria. For Menahem the son of Gadi went up from Tirzah, and came to Samaria, and smote Shallum the son of Jabesh in Samaria, and slew him, and reigned in his stead. And the rest of the acts of

King/Ruler	High Place/ System Destroyed?	Scripture
		Shallum, and his conspiracy which he made, behold, they are written in the book of the chronicles of the kings of Israel.
Menahem Evil	No	**2 Kings 15:17-18:** In the nine and thirtieth year of Azariah king of Judah began Menahem the son of Gadi to reign over Israel, and reigned ten years in Samaria. And he did that which was evil in the sight of the LORD: he departed not all his days from the sins of Jeroboam the son of Nebat, who made Israel to sin.
Pekahiah Evil	No	**2 Kings 15:23-24:** In the fiftieth year of Azariah king of Judah Pekahiah the son of Menahem began to reign over Israel in Samaria, and reigned two years. And he did that which was evil in the sight of the LORD: he departed not from the sins of Jeroboam the son of Nebat, who made Israel to sin.
Pekah Evil	No	**2 Kings 15:27-28:** In the two and fiftieth year of Azariah king of Judah Pekah the son of Remaliah began to reign over Israel in Samaria, and reigned twenty years. And he did that which was evil in the sight of the LORD: he departed not from the sins of Jeroboam the son of Nebat, who made Israel to sin.
Hoshea Evil	No	**2 Kings 17:1-2:** In the twelfth year of Ahaz king of Judah began Hoshea the son of Elah to reign in Samaria over Israel nine years. And he did that which was evil in the sight of the LORD, but not as the kings of Israel that were before him.

Because Israel would not turn away from their idolatry, God turned them over to a reprobate mind. They were taken into exile. To read the story, turn to 2 Kings 17 and read verses 5 through 23.

The reason I created the chart above is I wanted to show you what happens when a new system is not put in place. Israel's unwillingness to restore the altar of God cost them dearly.

Judah would follow in Israel's footsteps, refusing to destroy the demonic systems that had been put in place. Again, Israel was taken into exile, where they remained for about seventy years. A generation is thirty years; this means that Israel stayed in captivity to Babylon for more than two generations. The altar of God was not restored until between 537 and 536 BC after many of the Jews had been returned from Exile. By this time, they understood what needed to be done. They had to build an altar for the Lord, and then, they needed to build a temple for the Lord. Ezra 3:1-7 reads, "And when the seventh month was come, and the children of Israel were in the cities, the people gathered themselves together as one man to Jerusalem. Then stood up Jeshua the son of Jozadak, and his brethren the priests, and Zerubbabel the son of Shealtiel, and his brethren, and builded the altar of the God of Israel, to offer burnt offerings thereon, as it is written in the law of Moses the man of God. And they set the altar upon his bases; for fear was upon them because of the people of those countries: and they offered burnt offerings thereon unto the LORD, even burnt offerings morning and evening. They kept also the feast of tabernacles, as it is written, and offered the daily burnt offerings by number, according to the custom, as the duty of every day required; And afterward offered the continual burnt offering, both of the new moons, and of all the set feasts of the LORD that were consecrated, and of every one that willingly offered a freewill offering unto the LORD. From the first day of the seventh month began they to offer burnt offerings unto the LORD. But the foundation of the temple of the LORD was not yet laid. They gave money also unto the masons, and to the carpenters; and meat, and drink, and oil, unto them of Zidon, and to them of Tyre, to bring cedar trees from Lebanon to the sea of Joppa, according to the grant that they had of Cyrus king of Persia."

A Jewish leader by the name of Nehemiah supervised the rebuilding of Jerusalem after he had been released from captivity. Building the altar and the temple was just the beginning. Eventually a wall had to be erected; this represents fortification. Every prophet, every church, every organization and every community has to protect whatever it is that he or she has built. Proverbs 25:28 says it this way, "He that hath no rule over his own spirit is like a city that is broken down, and without walls." A city without walls is a place that's open for attack; it is a place that has no established boundaries or standards. This is a place that has no architect or prophetic vision to guide them. Proverbs 29:18 says it this way, "Where there is no vision, the people perish: but he that keepeth the law, happy is he."

To build, prophets have to work with Apostles—there is no getting around this! As a prophet or prophetic model of today, you have to partner with other leaders to accomplish your assignment. Again, you can't throw down a system without building a new one! This is why we see the same folks at the altar every Sunday; they had truly been set free, but the castle or, better yet, the temple remained empty! Somebody has to sit on the throne of their hearts! The

Prophetic Functions

new altars establish a new system, but the erection of the temple gives God back His seat of authority! And finally, they have to fortify their belief systems; they have to guard their hearts! This means that they can't continue doing what they were doing before they got bound; they can't continue operating in the same mindset that they were operating in before they got bound! This is why the teacher is so important! The teacher helps to build the wall!

Function Six: To Plant

Nehemiah 7:5: And my God put into mine heart to gather together the nobles, and the rulers, and the people, that they might be reckoned by genealogy.

After the temple had been built and the walls had been set in place, the priests, the Levites and the temple servants were put in place. These people represented the first-fruits. They led the people into repentance and helped to restore and facilitate the worship of YAHWEH. In the book of Nehemiah, you'll see all of the feasts being restored, the offices being restored, the tithes being restored and the Sabbath was restored.

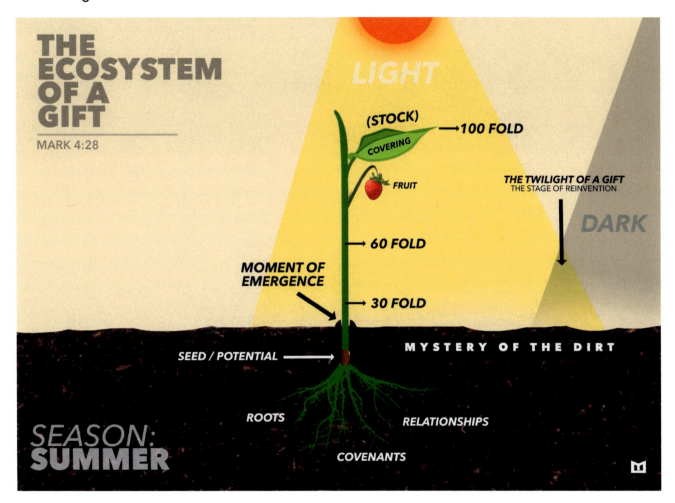

To plant means to raise up and restore leaders who may be in captivity because of fear. Elijah allowed fear to chase him into a cave, and because of this, he had to sow a seed. He had to raise up a replacement for himself; that replacement, of course, was the prophet Elisha. Some prophets plant churches, while others simply restore people. Hear me—this doesn't mean that every prophet should be ordaining people! Some prophets do set people in ministerial offices, for example, Elisha anointed Jehu king over Israel, Samuel anointed Saul king over Israel and Samuel would eventually anoint David as king over Israel. But all prophets are not set in place to ordain others. For example, John, the Baptist, didn't ordain people. He baptized people, but he did not ordain them! Prophets and prophetic types can and do, however, restore people! Sometimes, planting a seed can be as simple as giving someone a prophetic word or a word of knowledge! 1 Corinthians 14:24-25 says, "But if all prophesy, and there come in one that believeth not, or one unlearned, he is convinced of all, he is judged of all: And thus are the secrets of his heart made manifest; and so falling down on his face he will worship God, and report that God is in you of a truth."

The goal is to set people in place to sustain the system of God's Kingdom; this can be done on a corporate level or an individual level. Below, you'll find a chart detailing the many functions of a prophet.

Functions (Chart)				
Activator	Decoder	Hearer	Nurturer	Scribe
Advisor	Defender	Heart of God	Orator	Seer
Advocate	Deliverer	Herald	Partisan	Servant
Altar Builder	Designer	Incubator	Pattern	Sharer
Analyzer	Devotee	Influencer	Patron	Sifter
Announcer	Director	Inspirer	Peace-Maker	Son
Arbitrator	Disciple	Instigator	Perceptionist	Smoke Detector
Articulator	Dispatcher	Intercessor	Predictor	Sniper
Backer	Dissector	Interpreter	Preparer	Solutionist
Bearer	Diviner	Interventionist	Preserver	Spark
Birther	Dreamer	Intuitivist	Proclaimer	Spokesman
Builder	Edifier	Judge	Prognosticator	Steward
Calibrator	Expounder	Keeper	Promoter	Supporter
Change Agent	Eyes	Leader	Proponent	Surveyor
Cohort	Face Dweller	Liberator	Protector	Transformer
Commentator	Fire Starter	Linker	Psalmist	Translator
Communicator	Follower	Magi	Reconciler	Truth Specialist

Prophetic Functions

Conformer	Forecaster	Marksman	Releaser	Upholder
Confronter	Foreseer	Mediator	Resolver	Vaticinator
Connector	Forth-teller	Merger	Restorer	Visionary
Consultant	Friend of God	Midwife	Revelator	Warrior
Courier	Futurist	Minstrel	Revolutionist	Watchman
Creator	Glory Carrier	Model	Safeguard	Waterer
Custodian	Guard	Mouthpiece	Salvager	Womb
Decipher	Guide	Negotiator	Satellite	Vindicator

Prophetic Activation

Today is pull down, build up day! This activation is going to stretch you, but if you'll take the challenge, you will see why this activation is so important! Today, pull down your fears of building a business or writing a book! No excuses whatsoever! If you have a business idea, create a business plan! It needs to be detailed! Include the name or proposed name of your business and the projected launch date. If God has given you a book, open a document and create three pages for your book today! Create the cover with the book's title, the table of content and the first page of text! Again, no excuses!

Mission Four

T-06

Terraforming the Man

The world of astronomy (not to be confused with astrology) has always been an intriguing world for mankind. Our fascination with outer space and the unknown is linked to our curiosity regarding the supernatural. Since the beginning of time, mankind has always looked above his head and wondered what's beyond the stars. Does space have an end or an edge to it? Is there life on other planets? Why is space black? Our curiosity has caused us to write nursery rhymes like "Twinkle, Twinkle Little Star" and "Star Light, Star Bright." These songs were designed to engage our young and innocent imaginations—imaginations that had not yet been littered with doubt and unbelief. As we got older, our curiosity only seemed to grow as our imaginations continued to expand. We then started creating movies like "Planet of the Apes" and "Star Wars." Our imaginations and curiosity made room for a rare breed of humans to emerge; these people are called "creatives."

A creative, in simplistic terms, is a person who creates; it is a person who's creative abilities have been transported from one world (his or her imaginations) and made manifest in our world for others to see and benefit from. It's important to understand that everyone on the face of this planet is creative (adjective), but not everyone is a creative (noun). The difference between the two is called investment (action and energy). When a person who is creative begins to create (verb), that person then becomes a creative. Think of it this way—not everyone who says "Lord, Lord" is saved; Jesus said it this way, "Not everyone who says to me, 'Lord, Lord,' will enter the kingdom of heaven, but only the one *who does* the will of my Father who is in heaven." In other words, the life force that empowers faith is called "doing." Simply put, in order for something to be transported or transferred between two worlds, one of the resources of each world must be applied. Energy is a resource in the natural world. A thought is a resource in the supernatural world. When we put energy and effort behind a thought, we become conduits, transferring the wealth of one world into our own. Get this—every human on the face of this planet has potential, but potential is nothing but power stored in another dimension. That power has to be transferred between both dimensions in order for a person to become potent or powerful. For example, a battery becomes a battery the minute power is transferred into it. Before the transfer, it is nothing but a chiseled hunk of metal. It looks like a battery, but it has no power. Hear me—without power, it cannot *legally* be classified as a battery! This is why Timothy said that in the last days, men would have a *form* of godliness, but deny the power thereof. What does this mean? It means that men and women will arise and call themselves Christians; they will look and sound powerful, but they will be impotent. Just like a court of law, the Kingdom of God is backed by evidence! James 2:18-26 sums it up nicely; it reads, "Yea, a man may say, Thou hast faith, and I have works: shew me thy faith without thy works, and I will shew thee my faith by my works. Thou believest that there is one God; thou doest well: the devils also believe, and tremble. But wilt thou know, O vain man, that faith without works is dead? Was not Abraham our father justified by works, when he had offered Isaac his son upon the altar? Seest thou how faith wrought with his works, and by works was faith made perfect? And the scripture was fulfilled which saith, Abraham believed God, and it was imputed unto him for righteousness: and he was called the Friend of God. Ye see then how that by works a man is justified, and not by faith only. Likewise, also was not Rahab the harlot justified by works, when she had received the messengers, and had sent them out another way? For as the body without the spirit is dead, so faith without works is dead also."

We were made in the image of God. This means that He has given us the ability to "do" what He has done. The Creator communicates with us and this is what gives us the power and the ability to be creative. But to access this power, we have to use a natural resource of our own; again, it's called energy and effort. For example, if God gives you an idea about an invention, that idea has to be transferred from the thought realm into the natural realm. To do this, you can't just talk about your idea. You have to invest in it. You'd pay someone to draw your idea, you'd pay for the materials to create your idea, you'd pay someone to create your idea, you'd pay to have the idea tested, you'd pay to have the idea patented. But this money didn't just fall from the sky. You had to work for it! You had to invest time and energy into creating or sustaining someone else's idea, whether that idea was flipping burgers or performing brain surgery! This means that investing in someone else's ideas gives you the financial ability to manifest your own! The minute you manifest your idea and people begin benefiting from it, you have gone from being creative to being a creative. Think about it—we all know someone who is incredibly creative; they have creative abilities and they may even manifest some of those abilities and show them to you. This means that they are creative; they only become power-filled or powerful when they share what they've created with the world and the world starts benefiting from their creation.

Formula	Creator	Creature	Creative	Creativity	Recreate	Procreate

We are creative because we were created by the Creator of the Universe. This is why we don't worship the hosts of heaven or the universe itself; we worship YAHWEH, the Creator of all things, including Heaven and Earth.

Fact or False? Creatives are either prophets or a prophetic people.

It's a fact! It's important to note that the majority of creatives are prophetic, however, they are not all prophets. The reason I wanted to place emphasis on this is because it is dangerously common for prophetic people or creatives to believe themselves to be prophets. This is dangerous because many creatives take off their assigned mantles and attempt to wear mantles, titles and assignments that they haven't been graced to wear. This is largely due to a lack of understanding and a lack of teaching about the world of the prophetic. For example, when Saul gave David his armor to fight Goliath in, the scriptures tell us that David took it off. This is because David understood that the battle he was about to face was not his; it was the Lord's. This meant that the weapons of his warfare could not be carnal. In the natural, David defeated Goliath with a sling and a rock, but the Bible says there was no sword in the hand of David. This is because the sword was in his mouth. In other words, God defeated Goliath, David just got the credit!

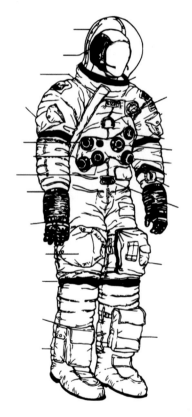

David was an astronaut in his era; he moved from one world to another. He started off as a shepherd; he spoke the language of a shepherd and invested time and energy tending to his father's sheep. In an instant, he found himself in a spacesuit—he found himself wearing Saul's armor about to fight a beast of a man. But the spacesuit that Saul had given him was not conducive for the fight that he was about to enter. He had to put on the full armor of God. What would you need to survive space travel? What would you need to survive on a planet that doesn't have oxygen or H20? You need to have a spacesuit; the scripture calls it the armor of God. For example, NASA has three types of spacesuits, all of which serve a unique purpose. They are:

- **IVA (Intravehicular Activity):** meant to be worn inside an aircraft; is more comfortable than any other spacesuit.
- **EVA (Extravehicular Activity):** meant to be worn outside an aircraft when astronauts explore other planets or take spacewalks.
- **IEVA (Intra/Extravehicular Activity):** meant to be worn inside and outside of a spacecraft; they protect astronauts from extreme temperature changes and micrometeorites.

The reason this information is important is because the natural realm gives us a synopsis or a snapshot of what's going on in the spiritual realm. This is why it was necessary for David to take off Saul's armor. Saul's armor was the equivalent of an EVA suit—a suit designed to be worn outside the will of God; this is what Saul placed his trust in, and because of this, Saul would eventually be killed wearing this very suit. David, on the other hand, placed his trust in God. He didn't need natural protection; he needed divine intervention. Again, he had to put on the full armor of God. The same is true for prophets and prophetic models (creatives). This is because the world of prophecy and creativity is a supernatural place where gravity doesn't exist. To understand this, you have to understand gravity. In the world of physics, gravity is the natural force that causes things to fall toward the earth. In other words, gravity deals with the natural realm; it is the force that gives weight to physical objects on our planet. It is a law in the natural, but that law has no jurisdiction in the spirit realm. Prophecy and creativity are both supernatural forces that enter our worlds through prophets and prophetic models (creatives). But before God transforms someone who is creative into a prophetic model (creative) or before God releases a prophet into the office of a prophet, He has to first terraform or transform the mind of that person. Think of your mind as a world within itself, and God's mind is a world within Himself. To get information to you, God has to first condition your world (mind).

Formula	Form	Conform	Inform	Reform	Transform	Terraform

First and foremost, what is terraforming? Wikitionary defines it this way, "The hypothetical process of deliberately modifying the atmosphere, temperature, surface topography or ecology of a planet, moon, etc. to make it similar to those of Earth and thus suitable for human life." In short, terraforming is colonizing a planet or making it inhabitable for humans. For example, scientists have considered terraforming the planet Mars; this would have been expensive and risky, so they settled on the concept of terraforming the moon. The idea is to turn the moon into a smaller version of Earth. Scientist believe that this is possible. Check out the article entitled, "What Would It Take to Terraform the Moon?" It reads, "To do that, we'd need to bombard our Moon with a hundred water-ice comets. Iceteroids. We'd find them flying all around the Earth. These comets would crush into Moon's surface. They'd fill the Moon's plains with water and disperse carbon dioxide along with water vapor and a little bit of ammonia and methane. All these gases would gather near the surface creating an atmosphere. The newly formed seas would reflect much more sunlight, making the Moon appear five times brighter if observed from Earth. Those iceteroids would also give Moon a momentum—they'd make our satellite spin close to an Earth-like cycle.

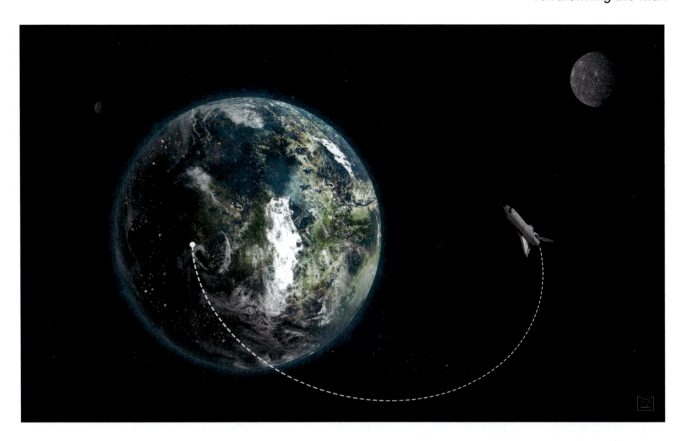

The more comets we batter into the Moon, the faster it would rotate. A lunar day would drop down from incredible 28 earth days to just 60 hours. Since our satellite wouldn't rotate on its axis at the same rate as it orbits the Earth anymore, it would no longer be tidally locked to our planet. For the earthers, this would mean we'd be able to see the dark side of the Moon, although, it wouldn't be dark. But how do we save the newly built lunar atmosphere from being stripped away by solar winds? We'd have a couple options. The first one is easy— Moon's own rotation would generate a dynamo effect. That dynamo could awaken Moon's once active magnetic field that would keep the atmosphere in place. If that doesn't work out, we would have to place a gigantic shield in the orbit. That shield would work as an artificial bow shock, making up for a missing magnetic field. When that's all sorted, we'd bring in genetically engineered plants suitable for growing on Moon's stony grime. We'd also drop some algae that would release oxygen into the air. That would be the start of the life on Moon.

Finally, after many decades of hard and costly work, we'd send the first human colony to settle down on a first man-made planet. The terraformed Moon would get very warm from greenhouse effects. It would be mostly cloudy, too, and with tides as high as 20 meters (65 feet). Surfers might want to check that out" (Source: Insh.com/What Would It Take to Terraform the Moon?/Robin Mel).

The author of the aforementioned article is describing what it would take to terraform the moon or make it inhabitable for humans. What the author is describing is how to turn one world into the image of another world. This is what terraforming is about; this is what transformation is about. It's about taking the atmosphere of one world and duplicating it in another world; this is what allows the vegetation that grows in one world to grow in another. Romans 12:2 states, "And be not conformed to this world: but be ye transformed by the renewing of your mind, that ye may prove what is that good, and acceptable, and perfect, will of God." Terraforming is about duplicating an atmosphere. Think of it this way, God wants to copy the atmosphere of Heaven and paste it here in the Earth; this way, His Kingdom will come and His will can be done in Earth as it is in Heaven.

When God made Adam's body, that was called terraformation. Get this—Adam wasn't just a person, he was a region. He was a garden within himself. Every word spoken to him was a seed that found its way into his heart and began to produce fruit in his life. This is why the Bible tells us to guard our hearts. This is also why God was able to pull Eve out of Adam. God created man in His image, and He created woman in the image of man. He produced mankind, and then, He told man to reproduce. When Adam sinned, he pretty much allowed his flesh and his mind to become fertile ground for the demonic world. This pretty much caused a split between both worlds (Heaven and Earth). Additionally, this created a communication gap between mankind and God. This is why God would later send Jesus to bridge the gap in communication, but before this could happen, He had to create prophets and prophetic models. The goal of the Old Testament prophet was to prepare the ground or, better yet, the hearts of man for Jesus' arrival. They had to act as spiritual astronauts, communicating the mind of God to His people. Today's prophets still do the same. They do this through:

Prophecy	Word of Wisdom
Word of Knowledge	Music
Dancing	Singing
Speaking	Drawing
Painting	Writing
Prophetic Movements	Crying
Building	Tearing Down
Laughing	Other Forms of Creative Expression

There are millions of ways that God expresses Himself through His sons and daughters; a prophetic expression can be something as simple as a hug or something as complex as a war declaration. And we all know that God can use anything and anyone, but the gravity of the

Kingdom is called trust! Consider the parable of the talents. Matthew 25:14-28 (ESV) reads, "For it will be like a man going on a journey, who called his servants and entrusted to them his property. To one he gave five talents, to another two, to another one, to each according to his ability. Then he went away. He who had received the five talents went at once and traded with them, and he made five talents more. So also, he who had the two talents made two talents more. But he who had received the one talent went and dug in the ground and hid his master's money. Now after a long time the master of those servants came and settled accounts with them. And he who had received the five talents came forward, bringing five talents more, saying, 'Master, you delivered to me five talents; here, I have made five talents more.' His master said to him, 'Well done, good and faithful servant. You have been faithful over a little; I will set you over much. Enter into the joy of your master.' And he also who had the two talents came forward, saying, 'Master, you delivered to me two talents; here, I have made two talents more.' His master said to him, 'Well done, good and faithful servant. You have been faithful over a little; I will set you over much. Enter into the joy of your master.' He also who had received the one talent came forward, saying, 'Master, I knew you to be a hard man, reaping where you did not sow, and gathering where you scattered no seed, so I was afraid, and I went and hid your talent in the ground. Here, you have what is yours.' But his master answered him, 'You wicked and slothful servant! You knew that I reap where I have not sown and gather where I scattered no seed? Then you ought to have invested my money with the bankers, and at my coming I should have received what was my own with interest. So take the talent from him and give it to him who has the ten talents."

Why did the master give one man five talents, but only give another man one talent? Think of it this way—every man, like Adam, is fertile ground; we are all gardens. We are tools of reproduction, but the problem is, when God gives us an ability or a responsibility, He plants certain strategies in our hearts. These strategies are called talents. But like a good gardener, He has to first consider the ground that He is about to plant these strategies in—is it fertile ground or is the ground barren? What's already growing in the ground? Each talent has a certain measure of weight and it comes with a certain measure of responsibility. Can the man or woman entrusted to keep the garden maintain it or would it be too much for the individual to bear? Get this—we are all individual gardens like the Garden of Eden. To get a better understanding of this, let's review Matthew 13:3-9; it reads, "And he spake many things unto them in parables, saying, Behold, a sower went forth to sow; and when he sowed, some seeds fell by the way side, and the fowls came and devoured them up: Some fell upon stony places, where they had not much earth: and forthwith they sprung up, because they had no deepness of earth: And when the sun was up, they were scorched; and because they had no root, they withered away. And some fell among thorns; and the thorns sprung up, and choked them: But other fell into good ground, and brought forth fruit, some an hundredfold, some sixtyfold, some thirtyfold. Who hath ears to hear, let him hear."

Please note that:
1. The sower is God.
2. The ground is the mind of man.
3. The fouls represent demonic spirits.
4. Stony places represent hard hearts.
5. Thorns represent bad company; another word for this is tares.
6. Good ground represents faith.

So, God went about sowing seeds; He gave one man five talents or five seeds, He gave another man two talents or two seeds, and He gave the last man a single talent or a single seed.

Prophets/Prophetic Models	Seeds/Talents	Status
Faithful, Mature Servant	5	Large Garden
Servant	2	Small Garden
Unfaithful, Immature Servant	1	Cemetery

The difference between a garden and a cemetery is one nourishes the living, while the other is a resting place for the dead. All of the men were prophets or prophetic models. They all had assignments; they were all supposed to act as gardens or places of reproduction. They were all supposed to act as representatives, but their first assignment was to allow God to change their minds. In other words, the first talent was about terraforming the man; it was centered around changing him from an unfaithful servant to a maturing one, and eventually, to a faithful servant. Howbeit, in order for this to happen, the man would have to sacrifice his will, his desires and his plans—he would have to till the ground that he was made from! He would have to till his flesh! Once the speck was removed from his eye, he could then begin to multiply himself. The second talent was about using the man to prepare someone else for terraformation. For example, after God created Adam, he didn't immediately give Adam a wife; He gave him an assignment. The scriptures tell us that He put Adam in the Garden to dress and keep it. After this, He gave Adam a commandment. He said, "Of every tree of the garden thou mayest freely eat: But of the tree of the knowledge of good and evil, thou shalt not eat of it: for in the day that thou eatest thereof thou shalt surely die." Hear me—a commandment is a boundary; it is a standard! What this literally means is that God gave Adam standards before He gave him a wife! What was He doing? He was terraforming the ground of Adam's heart! After this was done, God still didn't give Adam a help meet; instead, He gave him an assignment. Genesis 2:18-20 says, "And the LORD God said, It is not good that the man should be alone; I will make him an help meet for him. And out of the ground the LORD God formed every beast of the field, and every fowl of the air; and brought them unto Adam to see what he would call them: and whatsoever Adam called every living creature, that was the name thereof. And Adam gave names to all cattle, and to the fowl of the air, and to every beast of the field; but for Adam there was not found an help meet for him."

By this time, Adam had already been placed in the Garden to dress and keep it. He'd already been given a commandment, a standard or a boundary. When God looked upon him, He said, "It is not good for man to be alone. I will make a help meet for him." After this, God didn't immediately give Adam a wife; this is because God can see a need in your life, but before He gives you what you want and need, He has to create an atmosphere for you to sustain it! So, He took the same ground that Adam had been made of and pulled a bunch of animals out of it! Hear me—the second stage of readiness is deliverance! This is when God pulls the beasts out of you; this is when God has you to identify your own issues by name! This is called accountability! This is when you can look at lust and call it by its name; this is when you can look at unforgiveness, pride and rejection and call them by their names! Get this—this is when you can look at ambition and call it by its name! This is a part of the terraformation process! Remember, terraformation is the hypothetical process of deliberately modifying an atmosphere so that it can be similar to another one; this allows others who wouldn't normally be able to thrive in that atmosphere to survive and prosper there. Your attitude is the atmosphere of your personality! In other words, this is when God changes your character so that you'll know how to build and maintain healthy relationships! Once Adam's heart began to look like God's heart, He then pulled Eve out of Adam. Now, Adam, the maturing servant, had two talents—he had himself and his wife! This is a picture of what it means to be talented.

You are an astronaut. Your job is to deliver the goods from one world to another, but in order to do this, you have to allow God to mold and shape you into the image of Christ. Of course, the gifts and callings are without repentance! I'm not talking about your works, I'm dealing with your heart! Regardless of what condition you're in, what state you're in or what mindset you have, God can and will still use you! But the more you begin to look like Him, the more you begin to sound like Him and the more you begin to think like Him, the bigger your garden will get and the more that everything and everyone planted in your garden will grow! This means that He can trust you with more souls, He can trust you with more wealth and He can trust you with more notoriety. Again, trust is a currency that is accepted in both the Kingdom and the Earth.

You are not just a garden, you are a transportable garden, and in your belly, there are many seeds. But in order for those trees to produce fruit, you have to be in the right atmosphere and the ground has to be fertile. In order for the ground to be fertile, it has to be cultivated or turned. This process can be arduous, and this process can be taxing; this is because when ground is being cultivated or turned, everything that lives immediately beneath the surface will begin to manifest itself! This is why prophets can't be afraid to get their hands dirty; this is why creatives can't be intimidated by deliverance! Once the ground is turned, the seeds can be sown. These are the ideas that God gives you, and these are the souls that God entrusts you with. Each seed has to receive the right amount of light (revelation) and heat (love). Each seed needs to be watered; water, in the scriptures, represents baptism, the Holy Spirit and the Word of God. Once you allow God to terraform or transform you, He will use you to do the same for others. This is when you'll graduate from being a servant to a faithful servant! And this is when you'll be ready to ascend the hill of the Lord to ultimately become a son!

Prophetic Activation

It's time to terraform your life! List five problem areas of your life and create a plan to transform those areas. This is like a business plan, but it's personal! If you can't think of five issues that need to be addressed, ask some of the people closest to you! Don't skip this assignment!

Mission Five

T-05

Terraforming the Mountain

Psalm 24:3-6 reads, "Who shall ascend into the hill of the Lord? Or who shall stand in his holy place? He that hath clean hands, and a pure heart; who hath not lifted up his soul unto vanity, nor sworn deceitfully. He shall receive the blessing from the Lord, and righteousness from the God of his salvation. This is the generation of them that seek him, that seek thy face, O Jacob. Selah."

Other translations say the "mountain" of the Lord. In the previous chapter, we discussed terraforming the man, and now, your next set of instructions is to terraform one of the seven mountains of societal influence; they are:

1. Religion
2. Family
3. Government
4. Education
5. Business
6. Media
7. Arts and Entertainment

Each of these mountains represent collective belief systems. For example, there are over 4,200 religions in this world, with Christianity taking the lead as the largest religion, followed by Islam. Christianity is divided between Eastern and Western theology, and in these two kingdoms, there are six branches: Catholicism, Protestantism, Eastern Orthodoxy, Anglicanism, Oriental Orthodoxy, and Assyrians. Additionally, there are sixty denominations. Each of these faiths have individual sides (beliefs) and slopes (sects and denominations); all of them have their own individual peaks. Since the mountain belongs to the Lord, the large majority of these faiths are at the bottom of this mountain. The number of people who support each religion represents the height, width and length of each side. This is because we are all made of sand; we are all a part of the mountain. God said to Abraham, "I will surely bless you, and I will surely multiply your offspring as the stars of heaven and as the sand that is on the seashore." So, the Mountain of Religion, like every other mountain, is a pile of collective beliefs. To get a better understanding, check out the following chart.

Religion	Followers/Adherents
Christianity	2.4 Billion
Islam	1.9 Billion
Non-Religious (Secular) Agnostic/Atheist	1.2 Billion
Hinduism	1.15 Billion
Buddhism	521 Million
Chinese Traditional	394 Million
Ethnic	300 Million
African Traditional	100 Million
Sikhism	30 Million
Spiritism	15 Million
Judaism	14.5 Million
Bahá'í	7 Million

The Kingdom of God rests at the top of each mountain; this is why every knee shall bow and every tongue shall confess that Jesus Christ is Lord.

On these mountains, there are levels and legalities; there are also rulers, governors and laws that govern each level. Prophets terraform each of these kingdoms. They don't make them inhabitable for human existence and sustenance—God has already done this—prophets condition these worlds for Kingdom expansion and dominion. Genesis 1:26-27 gives us insight into God's heart regarding our purpose; it reads, "And God said, Let us make man in our image, after our likeness: and let them have dominion over the fish of the sea, and over the fowl of the air, and over the cattle, and over all the earth, and over every creeping thing that creepeth upon the earth. So God created man in his own image, in the image of God created he him; male and female created he them." We are designed to have and exercise dominion over each of these mountains. To get more understanding, let's inspect the word "dominion." The word "dominion" comes from the word "domain." Merriam Webster defines "domain" this way:
- complete and absolute ownership of land
- a sphere of knowledge, influence, or activity

The Greek word for "dominion" is "kuriotés" and it literally means to exercise lordship over something. Strong's Concordance defines it this way: "divine or angelic lordship, domination, dignity, usually with reference to a celestial hierarchy." The word "lordship" means supreme power or rule, so God gave mankind supreme power and authority over all the Earth and every living thing in it. This is natural authority. Jesus would later give us the keys to the supernatural world—keys represent legal access. In other words, Jesus gave us spiritual authority. Luke 10:19 reads, "Behold, I give unto you power to tread on serpents and scorpions, and over all the power of the enemy: and nothing shall by any means hurt you." When God gave mankind dominion over the Earth and everything in it, He pretty much gave us a set of crowns, but when Adam and Eve transgressed against the Lord, they turned over their keys and their crowns to death and hell. I won't be too expansive on this, but in short, Jesus took back the keys, but He didn't give them to all of mankind—He gave these keys to everyone who believed upon His name and confessed Him as Lord and Savior over their lives. This finalized His work, but not ours. We still had and have work to do; this is why the scriptures tell us to be "doers" of the Word and not hearers only. In other words, don't just have an ear to hear, but believers must also sacrifice their will so that God's will can be done. So, the first level of dominion that we have to exercise is called self-control. We are piles of dirt; we are individual mountains of influence, but before we can influence the world or anyone for that matter, we have to wrestle with our own sin nature; we have to overcome or terraform ourselves. Jesus said it this way, "Judge not, that ye be not judged. For with what judgment ye judge, ye shall be judged: and with what measure ye mete, it shall be measured to you again. And why beholdest thou the mote that is in thy brother's eye, but considerest not the beam that is in thine own eye? Or how wilt thou say to thy brother, Let me pull out the mote out of thine eye; and, behold, a beam is in thine own eye? Thou hypocrite, first cast out the beam out of thine own eye; and then shalt thou see clearly to cast out the mote out of thy brother's eye" (Matthew 7:1-5). This has been one of the most misinterpreted scriptures in the biblical text! Hear me—God wasn't saying that we could not judge one another! This scripture deals with hypocrisy! What He's literally saying is, don't judge a tree for bearing the same fruit that you're bearing! If you struggle with lust, don't judge someone else who's struggling with lust just because they're freakier than you are! Don't try to cast a devil out of someone when you are bound by that same devil! It's hypocrisy! The word "hypocrisy" is mentioned forty times in the Bible; Jesus spoke more about hypocrisy than any other sin. The Greek word for "hypocrisy" is "hypokrisis," and it literally means "actor." In other words, don't "act" like you have your life together when you don't!

Again, the first mountain of influence that we have to exercise dominion over is ourselves. This is what qualifies us to ascend the seven Mountains of Influence. Consider the life of Joseph. He was a prideful young man, howbeit, he had favor with his father. Genesis 37:3 reads, "Now

Israel loved Joseph more than all his children, because he was the son of his old age: and he made him a coat of many colours." This was favor! Favor is a technology of divine weaponry, but Joseph was too young and too immature to understand or manage the favor that was on his life. Galatians 4:1-2 reads, "Now I say, That the heir, as long as he is a child, differeth nothing from a servant, though he be lord of all; but is under tutors and governors until the time appointed of the father." The coat that Jacob gave Joseph represented a mantle. When he gave Joseph a coat of many colors, what this means is, he gave him a coat of many different fabrics and many different textures. Jacob's ability to weave together different seasons of his life was so amazing that you could not tell where one fabric of Joseph's garment ended and another began! He weaved them together masterfully and effortlessly by the wisdom of God. Every occupation had a uniform, so Joseph's coat was made of many different uniforms. In other words, his garment gave him access into many different worlds, vocations, occupations and opportunities.

Once Joseph got his coat, he started having dreams. Joseph's pride and his immaturity showed up when he started sharing his dreams with other people. Anytime God tells you something or shows you something, the revelation that He gives you needs to sit in your belly until it matures. In other words, you have to fully digest it and pull out all of its nutrients. Additionally, you have to break your dreams down into stages; the scriptures tell us that God knows the beginning from the end. God normally shows you the end. Remember this key—your dream will always take longer than you anticipate and cost more than you estimate. Let's look at Joseph's dilemma up close. Genesis 37:5-8 reads, "And Joseph dreamed a dream, and he told it his brethren: and they hated him yet the more. And he said unto them, Hear, I pray you, this dream which I have dreamed: For, behold, we were binding sheaves in the field, and, lo, my sheaf arose, and also stood upright; and, behold, your sheaves stood round about, and made obeisance to my sheaf. And his brethren said to him, Shalt thou indeed reign over us? Or shalt thou indeed have dominion over us? And they hated him yet the more for his dreams, and for his words."

What we see here is what appears to be the start of Joseph's decline, but what if I told you that what looks like a decline to us is actually an incline in the Kingdom? Joseph had been given the task of monitoring his brothers' activities, but the problem with this was, Joseph was still a young star; he was still immature and full of youthful pride. He wasn't a bad kid, he simply hadn't matured yet. He didn't yet understand the weight of his words or the complexity of his calling. He had been called to the Mountain of Government, but before he could ascend this mountain, he had to mature. He had to be terraformed or transformed by the renewing of his mind. He was a young star; in the world of astronomy, a young star is called a protostar.

According to Dictionary.com, a protostar is "an early stage in the evolution of a star, after the beginning of the collapse of the gas cloud from which it is formed, but before sufficient contraction has occurred to permit initiation of nuclear reactions at its core."

Facts About Protostars	Correlating Facts About Joseph
A protostar is a young star in the earliest stage of stellar evolution.	Joseph, like everyone else, started off as a young star. In Genesis 37, we see him during the infancy of his calling. He had already been entrusted with the responsibility of being an overseer; this was not the best position for him at that time because he was young, naive and immature. It's almost as if he had been entrusted to be his older brothers' pastor, and this would have been okay if Joseph was mature and experienced. Joseph was in his earliest stages of evolution; he needed to be hidden, he needed to be developed and he needed to be measured.
When a protostar is born, it spends most of its youth hidden in a molecular cloud.	Jacob's mistake was that he did not hide Joseph properly. This is likely because he didn't understand the weight, the call and the responsibility that was linked to his youngest son. Jacob was, in a sense, his son's pastor. Pastors have the difficult task of hiding or covering a gift until that gift is mature enough and strong enough to shine on its own. Just like the glory that covered Adam and Eve lifted the minute they'd sinned, the cloud that should have covered Joseph lifted before its time, revealing his idiosyncrasies. And just like Adam and Eve had been cast out of the Garden of Eden, Joseph was bound and cast out of his birthplace.
A protostar has to shrink in size in order to generate the energy it uses when it radiates.	Every star has to humble himself or herself. Humility allows a star to generate and preserve the energy that he or she will need later in life. This is why, contrary to unpopular

Facts About Protostars	Correlating Facts About Joseph
	belief, we need our pastors! Stars develop in the darkness; they perfect their glow when no one is looking! Burnout is usually the result of a star exhausting all of its energy before its time!
The shrinkage of a protostar increases the gravity of that star.	The gravity of a star represents the weight of that star. Every time an influencer, a gift or a prophetic model chooses to remain humble, God increases the influence and the size of that gift. In the Kingdom, the formula for greatness is meekness, and the formula for longevity is humility!
A new protostar does not shine.	There is a time, a moment and a season for everything; it is dangerous for a gift, a prodigy or a model to be revealed before his or her time. Immature prophets and prophetic models are often anxious and ready to reveal themselves and their gifts to the world, but this is why every gift needs a cloud or, better yet, a pastor. Every gift needs someone to cover him or her until the appointed season. Ecclesiastes 3:1-8 says, "To every thing there is a season, and a time to every purpose under the heaven: A time to be born, and a time to die; a time to plant, and a time to pluck up that which is planted; a time to kill, and a time to heal; a time to break down, and a time to build up; a time to weep, and a time to laugh; a time to mourn, and a time to dance; a time to cast away stones, and a time to gather stones together; a time to embrace, and a time to refrain from embracing; a time to get, and a time to lose; a time to keep, and a time to cast away; atime to rend, and a time to sew; a time to keep silence, and a time to speak; a time to love, and a time to hate; a time of war, and a

Facts About Protostars	Correlating Facts About Joseph
	time of peace."
A star doesn't shine until it completes the protostar stage.	Every star and every gift has to go through a process and Joseph was no different! He was anointed and he was called, but he wasn't yet ready to shine.

Joseph was a young star, but he needed to be developed before his light was revealed. He had favor with his father, Jacob, but favor in its infancy is called favoritism! Favoritism prematurely reveals the potential on a person's life; this is what puts them in danger! Joseph had to start at the bottom (humility) before he could assess the platforms (honor) he'd dreamed about. Let's look at Joseph's timeline.

Age	Joseph's Timeline of Events
17	Thrown in pit, sold into slavery
28	Potiphar's wife accuses Joseph; Joseph is imprisoned
30	Interprets Pharaoh's dreams; becomes second in command

When we look at the timeline of Joseph's life, we see what we interpret to be a decline, however, Joseph was really starting his ascension up the mountain he was called to. But before this could happen, he had to be developed in darkness. Every ounce of pride in him had to be squeezed out; every ounce of ambition in him had to be snatched out! In short, Joseph had to exercise dominion over his own carnality before he could began his ascension on the Mountain of Government. God used Joseph's experiences to transform him into the person he needed to be for the platform or world he needed to terraform. The same is true for you. What Mountain of Influence are you called to? What level of that mountain do you believe you're called to? And finally, what are you doing today to prepare for the assignment that God has entrusted you with? Are you running from your assignment like Jonah did or are you running towards your assignment like David did? Joseph was called to terraform the world of Egypt or, better yet, the systems in Egypt. He was sent into a pagan world, and his assignment was to change the atmosphere of that world; this way, he could prepare a place for his family during the famine. To get a better understanding of this presentation, let's look at the Cosmological Order of the Kingdom.

Cosmological Order of the Kingdom
Every world is made up of kingdoms
Every kingdom is divided into realms
Every realm is made up of dimensions
Every dimension is comprised of levels
Every level is accessed by doors
Every door is opened by keys

Every mountain represents a world; another word for world is "system." There's the world of faith, the world of anointing, the world of gifts, the world of praise/worship and the world of preaching. When we talk about a world, we're talking about a particular entity in its totality; we're talking about everything that belongs to that entity—all the branches, levels and everything that pertains to a specific entity. Every world is made up of kingdoms, for example, the many faiths of all kingdoms. There is the kingdom of Islam, the kingdom of Buddhism, the kingdom of Sikhism and so on. Every one of these kingdoms are subject to the Kingdom of YAHWEH. Every kingdom is divided into realms, for example, when dealing with the world of religion and the kingdom of Christianity, all of the denominations in Christianity represent realms. Next, every realm is made up of dimensions. A dimension is a world of thought; this represents the thinkers and the mindsets supporting each kingdom. For example, in the kingdom of Christianity, each realm would be comprised of doctrines, traditions and cultures; these are the dimensions. Every dimension is comprised of levels. These are the people who empower each kingdom, starting with the leaders, all the way down to the janitors. For example, if I'm the janitor for an organization, it is not my job to know the secrets of that organization, my job is to know where the trash is! I'm not demeaning any occupation; I just want to make a point. Every person on every level is needed to sustain that organization. Now, if I'm a janitor and I become disgruntled because I want to know what they're talking about in the boardroom, I could end up getting fired because I'm trying to think on a level that is locked to me or is off limits to me. If I came into an organization and started an entry level position, I couldn't just walk into a boardroom and start making decisions. In order for me to ascend the hill or get promoted into the boardroom, there are certain levels that I must master. If I'm struggling with punctuality, I don't have to worry about being promoted into a managerial position. I would have to master punctuality! I would have to make all of my deadlines; this is what would cause my superiors to trust me more with even bigger assignments, greater decisions and smaller deadlines. The bigger the assignment, the bigger the opportunity. It all starts with levels. I would have to master every level. Now, the only way I would have that position, I would have had to entered in through a door. Every level is accessed by doors. The door, in my case, may have been an employee. There are some jobs that you can't get hired with unless someone in that company recommends you. Your door could be your degree or your application. For the Mountain of Religion, your door could be, for example, your grandmother. Maybe she took you to church every Sunday when you were a child. Maybe, you were an exotic dancer and the door opened when someone you handed your business card to handed you his business card, and he turned out to be a pastor. So, you looked him up online, watched a few of his sermons and felt something in you stirring. Or the door could have been a book that you read. Maybe you were a proud atheist who'd purchased a book just to discredit it, but the author ended up dismantling and discrediting the lies you'd come to trust in. And finally, every door is opened by keys. Sometimes, a key is the right word in the right season.

To get a better understanding of the cosmological order of the kingdom, look at the chart below.

Kingdom	Realm	Dimension	Level	Door	Key
Man	Body	Mind	Conscious	Eyes	Time
	Soul	Will	Subconscious	Ears	Words
	Spirit	Emotions	Unconscious	Nose	Trauma
				Touch	Time
				Taste	Experience

As a creative, you are currently on one of the Mountains of Influence. Maybe you're at the bottom of the mountain or maybe you've already started ascending. You have friends on each mountain, all of which are on a certain level. This means they think a certain way. Maybe, you've already terraformed yourself; you've overcome the works of the flesh which, according to Galatians 5:19-21, are adultery, fornication, uncleanness, lasciviousness, idolatry, witchcraft, hatred, variance, emulations, wrath, strife, seditions, heresies, envyings, murders, drunkenness, revelings. You've studied the Word of God, learned to resist your lustful appetite and learned to prioritize the Word and will of God over your own opinion and will. And now, it's time for you to ascend the hill of the Lord, but you're having trouble with the level that you're on. Let's say, for example, that you hate your job, you don't get along with half of the people at your church and you're pretty much estranged from your family. Your natural human inclination would be to try to ascend each of these organizations so that you can platform your opinion. So, you may find yourself trying to get a promotion on your job, get into a leadership position at your church or set up a meeting with your family where you plan to list all of your grievances. But things don't work out the way you planned them to or in the time-frame you want them to work out. Your job doesn't promote you, but gives the management position to someone you dislike, your church decides that you're not ready to be ordained and your family has a list of grievances of their own. What is your next inclination? To withdraw yourself, of course. Now, you may find yourself planning to quit your job, find another church or disown your family. This may appear to work out for you for a few seasons, but one day, you'll come to realize that you're still in the same place and on the same level that you were a few years back. Most people don't realize that they're stuck until the people around them start ascending. What's the problem; why isn't there any movement in your life? It's simple. You had a job to do and you didn't complete it. Why would your job promote you to manager if you didn't complete an assignment or two that they gave you? Now, apply that principle to your faith! Why would God promote you to the next level when you haven't finished the assignment He gave you regarding the level that you're on? Another way to say this is—why would God give you access to the invention idea when you haven't even finished the book He gave you? The gravity of the Kingdom is trust, and if God can't trust you to terraform the level that you're on, He definitely can't trust you with greater levels.

Prophetic Activation

Today's activation is simple. List the Mountain *or* Mountains of Influence that you believe you're called to, and list three ways you plan to terraform those mountains.

Mission Six

T-04

Altitudinal Zonation

What is altitudinal zonation? Wikipedia defines it this way, "Altitudinal zonation or elevation zonation in mountainous regions describes the natural layering of ecosystems that occurs at distinct elevations due to varying environmental conditions. Temperature, humidity, soil composition, and solar radiation are important factors in determining altitudinal zones, which consequently support different vegetation and animal species. Altitudinal zonation was first hypothesized by geographer Alexander von Humboldt who noticed that temperature drops with increasing elevation." In layman's terms, altitudinal zonation deals with each zone or level of a mountain; it details:
1. the climate or atmosphere on each level
2. the type of vegetation that grows on each level
3. the animals that thrive on each level

Levels	Descriptions
Nival	Covered in snow throughout most of the year. Vegetation is extremely limited to only a few species that thrive on silica soils.
Alpine	The zone that stretches between the tree line and snowline. This zone is further broken down into Sub-Nival and Treeless Alpine (in the tropics-Tierra fria; low-alpine). • **Sub-nival:** The highest zone that vegetation typically exists. This area is shaped by the frequent frosts that restrict extensive plant colonization. Vegetation is patchy and is restricted to only the most favorable locations that are protected from the heavy winds that often characterize this area. Much of this region is patchy grassland, sedges and rush heaths typical of arctic zones. Snow is found in this region for part of the year. • **Treeless alpine (low-alpine):** Characterized by a closed carpet of vegetation that includes alpine meadows, shrubs and sporadic dwarfed trees. Because of the complete cover of vegetation, frost has less of an effect on this region, but due to the consistent freezing temperatures tree growth is severely limited.

Levels	Descriptions
Montane	Extends from the mid-elevation forests to the tree line. The exact level of the tree line varies with local climate, but typically the tree line is found where mean monthly soil temperatures never exceed 10.0 degrees C and the mean annual soil temperatures are around 6.7 degrees C. In the tropics, this region is typified by montane rain forest (above 3,000 ft) while at higher latitudes coniferous forests often dominate.
Lowland	This lowest section of mountains varies distinctly across climates and is referred to by a wide range of names depending on the surrounding landscape. Colline zones are found in tropical regions and Encinal zones and desert grasslands are found in desert regions. • **Colline (tropics):** Characterized by deciduous forests when in oceanic or moderately continental areas, and characterized by grassland in more continental regions. Extends from sea level to about 3,000 feet (roughly 900 m). Vegetation is abundant and dense. This zone is the typical base layer of tropical regions. • **Encinal (deserts):** Characterized by open evergreen oak forests and most common in desert regions. Evaporation and soil moisture control limitation of which encinal environments can thrive. Desert grasslands lie below encinal zones. Very commonly found in the Southwestern United States. • **Desert grassland:** Characterized by varying densities of low lying vegetation, grasslands zones cannot support trees due to extreme aridity. Some desert regions may support trees at base of mountains however, and thus distinct grasslands zones will not form in these areas.

Information on chart above was taken from Wikipedia

- Every level has an atmosphere or a climate.
- Every climate determines the type of vegetation that grows on each level.
- The vegetation that grows on each level will determine the types of animals and insects that live on each level.

The following information was taken from the World Atlas:

Factors Influencing Altitudinal Zonation	
Temperature	It is common knowledge that an increase in height comes with a reduction in temperature. Most vegetation relies on high temperature to thrive. Consequently, varying temperatures will have a direct impact on the length of time that plants can grow. Temperatures that are too high or two low support very few species of plants. The most vegetation is found in the tropical regions. Most of the huge coniferous and deciduous trees grow there. Zones with similar conditions will have bigger vegetation and vice versa.
Humidity	Humidity refers to the amount of water in the atmosphere. Things like the levels of evapotranspiration and precipitation fall here. Precipitation accounts for the highest quantity of humidity in the atmosphere. As such, precipitation is most important in determining zonation. As warm moist air rises up the mountain side, it reaches a height where it condenses and forms precipitation like rain. The middle parts of the mountain receive the highest amount of rainfall. As such, most flora and fauna is located there as opposed to other regions. Higher regions of the mountain experience very low temperatures. Vegetation found there has to be specially adapted to the extreme temperatures. Same applies to the lower and hotter regions.
Soil Composition	The type of soil in a zone will obviously affect the type and size of vegetation living there. It is also common knowledge that most plants will thrive in zones with richer soils. Nutrients come from minerals in rocks and decaying vegetation or animals. Highly fertile soil means richer plant and animal life. Example, the zones in tropical areas have fewer plant species on the ground level due to undergrowth and dead leaves.
Biological Factors	This refers to simple Darwinism. Stronger species will kill weaker ones. The weaker ones can either adapt or migrate. Example, the adaptation of weaker trees by growing around the trunks of bigger ones. It is crucial to remember that this factor is difficult to prove but academicians agree that it's a factor in zonation.
Solar Radiation	Most plants rely on the light from the sun to make food for their survival. Differing levels of sunlight lead to the creation of zones on the mountainside.

Altitudinal Zonation

Massenerhebung Effect	This means that the physical location of the mountain should be taken into account while attempting to determine zonation. The effect expects that zonation on lower mountains may mirror those of higher mountains with the zonation belts occurring at equally lower heights.

How do we apply this information to the Seven Mountains of Influence? Remember, every level has a climate. As a prophet or as a creative, you have to adjust to the temperatures on every level that you ascend to. Let's take the example we used earlier. If you're working at a job that you hate, your assignment isn't to quit the job and find a better one! Your assignment is to master your emotions in the climate that you're in! This means that you have to adapt to the people, the environment and everything that makes you uncomfortable. In short, you have to take dominion over yourself, so much so that you are no longer moved by the external factors! This means that you've terraformed your character, so now you can change the temperature of the place that you're in! Did you know that a prophet or a prophetic model has the ability to change the weather or the climate of a place? Let's look at the Prophet Elijah. 1 Kings 17:1 reads, "And Elijah the Tishbite, who was of the inhabitants of Gilead, said unto Ahab, As the LORD God of Israel liveth, before whom I stand, there shall not be dew nor rain these years, but according to my word." Elijah was so potent that he closed the windows of Heaven over Israel! Now, I'm not telling you to declare droughts and famines in the lives of your enemies, after all, this would be witchcraft! What I am saying is, you don't have to sit in a negative atmosphere and submit to it. As a believer, you have the power to force that atmosphere to submit to you! You do this by praying, prophesying over the place, and get this, by loving your enemies! You can't change an atmosphere if you hate the folks who are in it!

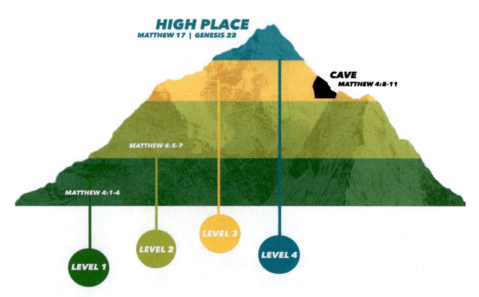

Once you've mastered the zone you're in, once you've terraformed the zone you're in, and once you've been transformed by the experience, God can promote you to a different level. Now, remember, on each level, there are different types of vegetation; this means that you will have to adjust your diet! You can't just read the Bible once a day anymore, you can't just pray for 15 minutes a day anymore and you can't just fast every six months! You have to increase your intake! This is why believers ascend, only to descend into depression. This is why believers get consumed with work, with bills and with common day to day problems. If your prayer time doesn't increase, you'll begin to decrease, which will cause your problems to appear to be bigger than they used to be! This is why so many creatives have gone to their graves, filled with the talents, the giftings and the assignments, all of which got buried with them.

The Elijah Model

2 Kings 2:1-11 reads, "And it came to pass, when the LORD would take up Elijah into heaven by a whirlwind, that Elijah went with Elisha from Gilgal. And Elijah said unto Elisha, Tarry here, I pray thee; for the LORD hath sent me to Bethel. And Elisha said unto him, As the LORD liveth, and as thy soul liveth, I will not leave thee. So they went down to Bethel. And the sons of the prophets that were at Bethel came forth to Elisha, and said unto him, Knowest thou that the LORD will take away thy master from thy head to day? And he said, Yea, I know it; hold ye your peace. And Elijah said unto him, Elisha, tarry here, I pray thee; for the LORD hath sent me to Jericho. And he said, As the LORD liveth, and as thy soul liveth, I will not leave thee. So they came to Jericho. And the sons of the prophets that were at Jericho came to Elisha, and said unto him, Knowest thou that the LORD will take away thy master from thy head today? And he answered, Yea, I know it; hold ye your peace. And Elijah said unto him, Tarry, I pray thee, here; for the LORD hath sent me to Jordan. And he said, As the LORD liveth, and as thy soul liveth, I will not leave thee. And they two went on. And fifty men of the sons of the prophets went and stood to view afar off: and they two stood by Jordan. And Elijah took his mantle, and wrapped it together, and smote the waters, and they were divided hither and thither, so that they two went over on dry ground. And it came to pass, when they were gone over, that Elijah said unto Elisha, Ask what I shall do for thee, before I be taken away from thee. And Elisha said, I pray thee, let a double portion of thy spirit be upon me. And he said, Thou hast asked a hard thing: nevertheless, if thou see me when I am taken from thee, it shall be so unto thee; but if not, it shall not be so. And it came to pass, as they still went on, and talked, that, behold, *there appeared* a chariot of fire, and horses of fire, and parted them both asunder; and Elijah went up by a whirlwind into heaven."

Elijah was at the top or peak of his life. He'd ascended the hill of the Lord; he'd accomplished the will of God for his life. And now, it was time for him to pass the baton or, better yet, his authority to his successor.

First Level/ Peak	Elijah
Second in Rank	Elisha
Third in Rank	The Prophets
Base Level	Sons of the Prophets

He couldn't just give this authority to any prophet or prophetic model. He had to impart this authority into the man who'd been following him closely; this was the third level of impartation. The first level was sacrifice; in order for Elisha to qualify to become a direct descendant of Elijah, he had to sacrifice his own will. He had to follow Elijah. The next level of impartation was wisdom. Elijah had to share his knowledge, his understanding and his wisdom with Elisha; this is what creates the capacity or the space needed for the third level of impartation to take place. The final level or peak level of impartation is authority. In order for Elisha to get Elijah's authority, he had to follow him closely. The sons of the prophets had been following Elijah, but they weren't following him as closely as Elisha had been, so they didn't qualify for the level of impartation that he gave to Elisha. This is why it's a dangerous and immature mistake for a prophet or prophetic model to rush towards the peak of any given organization! Power or authority without wisdom and development is the formula for pride! And according to Proverbs 16:18, "Pride goes before destruction, and a haughty spirit before a fall."

Before you attempt to ascend any of the Mountains of Influence, it is important that you not only have a mentor, but that your mentor crafts a specialized diet for you! For example, if you're called to the Mountain of Religion, your mentor may be your pastor. Every believer needs a pastor! Another word for pastor is shepherd. Without a shepherd, you'll foolishly wander into other zones that you aren't necessarily adapted for and you'll try to consume information that you don't have the teeth to chew or the wherewithal to digest. I don't say this to scare you, but to inform you—graveyards and mental institutions are filled with prophets and creatives who decided within themselves that they were called to do ministry all by themselves—without knowledge and without instruction! This is as dangerous as it is foolish! Because of the hurt, the rejection and the issues they've faced in their lives, they lost their ability to trust anyone, including God! Hear me—just because they still claim to be Christian, they build spooky websites and record doom and gloom videos on social media doesn't mean that they trust God! As a matter of fact, this is the evidence that they don't trust Him! They are trying to work their way into His favor when we are no longer under the law of works! This is why they are doom and gloom prophets; this is why they are triggered by everything they don't agree with that happens in the church! They believe that if they prophesy against the leaders that they don't agree with, that they'll somehow prove to God that they are for Him, but He doesn't need this! He just needs us to obey Him! That's it! Proverbs 11:14 warns us this way. "Where no counsel is, the people fall: but in the multitude of counselors there is safety." When a prophet or prophetic model tries to be a lone star, this is often the manifestation of hurt, rejection and pride! When these three toxins come together, they pervert prophets and believers, and cause them to hallucinate; they begin to think that they are hearing from God when they are not! This is the formula for rebellion; this is the potion for witchcraft! And if they try to involve themselves in a church, they don't stay long because they start dealing with confusion and hearing:

- "God said you've outgrown your pastor!"
- "God said it's time for you to leave your church!"
- "God said that you are a Joseph, and because of this, no one understands you, including your pastor!"
- "Your pastor doesn't understand the complexity of your anointing! You need to find another pastor or become your own pastor!"
- "God said that you are a David and your pastor is your Saul! It's time to run!"
- "Everybody is going to hell! It is your job to walk into churches, rebuke the leaders and warn the people!

These types of "messages" usually signal that the prophet or the prophetic model is under the influence of pride, hurt and rejection! Now, I'm not saying that there hasn't been instances where God has told someone to leave a church, but what I am saying is that these thoughts or "inner dialogues" are common with creatives who have wandered outside of their jurisdiction! Get this—the air on each level of a mountain is different. The higher you go, the thinner the air will be. This is what they refer to in the scientific realm as "altitude sickness." What is altitude sickness? "Altitude sickness, the mildest form being acute mountain sickness (AMS), is the negative health effect of high altitude, caused by rapid exposure to low amounts of oxygen at high elevation. Symptoms may include headaches, vomiting, tiredness, trouble sleeping, and dizziness. Acute mountain sickness can progress to high altitude pulmonary edema (HAPE) with associated shortness of breath or high altitude cerebral edema (HACE) with associated confusion. Chronic mountain sickness may occur after long term exposure to high altitude" (Source: Wikipedia/Altitude Sickness).

Hear me—when a leader gives you a mantle, that leader is clothing you with the authority you'll need for the range that you're on! Joseph's father knit a mantle for him, but he didn't pass his mantle to Joseph in that hour. He created one for him. This means that your leader knows what size mantle you should be wearing! Don't covet someone else's mantle or assignment, otherwise, you'll find yourself trying to fight devils that you aren't ready to fight; you'll try to battle temperatures that you haven't been conditioned to survive! Again, this is the recipe for a straitjacket! When your leader decides to pass his or her mantle, the person or people who'll get the mantle are normally the folks who followed the closest. This means that they didn't complain about how steep the mountain was or how cold the temperatures got. They didn't gossip about their leaders or leave their churches every time they got offended or felt overlooked! They followed closely, even when it didn't make sense to do so! They stayed when others left. What were they doing? Increasing their capacity!

Every zone of the mountain you're called to has a temperature. You will have to be conditioned for every level that you ascend to. This conditioning comes through prayer, fasting and mentorship. This conditioning prepares you to survive the cold fronts, the loneliness that ascending leaders and believers feel and the wild animals (devils and devil bound people) that you'll face as you ascend. The old folks used to say, "New level, new devil," and as simplistic as this statement is, as catchy as this statement is, it is actually true! Luke 12:48 states, "For unto whomsoever much is given, of him shall be much required: and to whom men have committed much, of him they will ask the more."

All the same, don't rush towards the spotlight; don't covet after platforms, titles or positions! When Satan wanted to get Eve outside the will of God, he simply tempted her with a new position. Genesis 3:1-5 reads, "He said to the woman, 'Did God actually say, 'You shall not eat of any tree in the garden?' And the woman said to the serpent, 'We may eat of the fruit of the trees in the garden, but God said, 'You shall not eat of the fruit of the tree that is in the midst of the garden, neither shall you touch it, lest you die.' But the serpent said to the woman, 'You will not surely die. For God knows that when you eat of it your eyes will be opened, and you will be like God, knowing good and evil.'" Eve's job was secure and her benefits were great! But one of the ways that Satan intoxicates believers is by feeding them lies and causing them to feel used or taken advantage of in their churches, on their jobs or in their relationships. When believers listen to the enemy's lies, they become so intoxicated with pride that they begin to lean to their own understanding! Genesis 3:6 says, "So when the woman saw that the tree was good for food, and that it was a delight to the eyes, and that the tree was to be desired to make one wise, she took of its fruit and ate..." What was she doing here? She was beginning to doubt God; this caused her to lean or depend on her own human reasoning. This is the same mistake that most believers make, especially creatives. In order for Eve to overcome the demonic winds of doctrine that were coming against her, she would have had to respect the position that she had, and more importantly, honor the One who gave her that position.

Legal Zoning

Gravity is a law. Let's look at a few definitions.
- **Law:** a general rule that states what always happens when the same conditions exist

(Source: Cambridge Dictionary).
- **Scientific Law:** Scientific laws or laws of science are statements, based on repeated experiments or observations, that describe or predict a range of natural phenomena (Source: Wikipedia).

Sir Isaac Newton was credited for discovering Newton's law of universal gravitation, also known as the law of gravity. According to Wikipedia, "Newton's law of universal gravitation is usually stated that every particle attracts every other particle in the universe with a force which is directly proportional to the product of their masses and inversely proportional to the square of the distance between their centers." In short, the law of gravity dictates that anything with mass that goes up (in the Earth realm) must come down. In the Earth, gravity pulls everything downward; it is the force that literally keeps us grounded. And get this—we have to respect every law that we come under. The only way to legally get around a law is to apply an even greater law. For example, Newton's published three laws of motion. They are:

Law	Statement	Interpretation
First Law of Motion	"A body at rest will remain at rest, and a body in motion will remain in motion unless it is acted upon by an external force."	This means that anything that has mass doesn't have the ability to move or change directions by itself; it has to be acted upon by an external force.
Second Law of Motion	"The force acting on an object is equal to the mass of that object times its acceleration."	The mathematical formula for this is $F = ma$: - F (force) - m (mass) - a (acceleration) In short, when a force acts upon a massive body, it causes that body to accelerate or change directions. What this literally means is any force applied to an object at rest causes the object to move or accelerate in the direction of the force. On the other hand, if the object is already moving or, better yet, in motion, that body might speed up, slow down, or change directions, but of course, this is dependent upon the direction of the force and the direction that the object and reference frame are moving relative to one other.

Law	Statement	Interpretation
Third Law of Motion	"For every action, there is an equal and opposite reaction."	This law pretty much details the relationship between two objects of mass; it details what happens between an object of mass or body when it moves upon or exerts force against another body. In layman's terms, when one body pushes against another body, the second body pushes back with the same amount of force.

Again, to get around one law, another law has to be applied. An object at rest must stay at rest; this is a law, but when acted upon by an external force equal to or greater than its mass, the object will respond. This is another law. The reason this information is important is because it helps us to understand the relationship between the natural realm and the spiritual realm. This is because what we see in the natural is nothing but an interpretation of what we can't see in the spirit. For example, a mountain climber has to understand the forces that he or she will be faced with when ascending a mountain. An astronaut must understand the forces that he or she will be faced with when traveling out of this world. Understanding the differences between two worlds, two levels or two planes is essential, otherwise, people will go to new heights or new places trying to apply laws to that place that are only applicable in the world or the region that they came out of! This is why there are so many believers still living in bondage to the Mosaic Law when Jesus has already come and set the captives free! This is also why our graveyards, asylums and prisons are overflowing with prophets and prophetic models. Think of it this way—as an American, you can't go into another country, break the laws of that country, and when they arrest or bind you, start to tell them that what you did is legal in the United States. American laws don't apply in that region, nor do they override their laws! So, for example, it is illegal to chew gum in Singapore (as silly as it sounds). The penalty for doing so for first time offenders is a prison sentence of up to two years and a fine of up to $100 thousand. This law applies to both tourists and citizens, so if you visit Singapore, it goes without saying that American's long arm of law can't reach or protect you. While in Singapore, you must abide by their laws and honor their culture! Again, anytime you go between two worlds, you must understand the laws of the world that you're entering and how those laws affect you. When going between two climates, you must understand the temperature of the climate that you're entering and how to dress, what to expect and what you'll need to take with you to survive in that atmosphere. What I'm trying to say is, as a prophet or creative-type, you will ascend one or more of the seven Mountains of Influence, but when you ascend, you need to be familiar with the next level and how to respond to it. This is the Law of Correct Response;

this law dictates that:
1. Everything that God does demands a response.
2. Everything that God has created demands a response when acted upon.

One amazing and often overlooked fact is, mankind has no dominion over the space realm. Once we leave Earth, we leave behind our domain and the laws of that domain. This means that we go outside of our dominion! Genesis 1:26-28 confirms this. In this scripture, we see God giving mankind a set of boundaries. The scripture reads, "Then God said, 'Let us make man in our image, after our likeness. And let them have dominion over the fish of the sea and over the birds of the heavens and over the livestock and over all the earth and over every creeping thing that creeps on the earth.' So God created man in his own image, in the image of God he created him; male and female he created them. And God blessed them. And God said to them, 'Be fruitful and multiply and fill the earth and subdue it, and have dominion over the fish of the sea and over the birds of the heavens and over every living thing that moves on the earth.'" This is the reason that man has not and cannot seem to travel too far in space or figure out most of the mysteries involving space. While space is interesting and it helps us to understand the Earth, we simply have no jurisdiction there! I'm not suggesting that we shouldn't do space travel; I think space travel is amazing! It's informative and it provokes us to be even more creative. What I am saying is, just like you shouldn't go to a foreign country if you are ignorant of that country's laws, we have to familiarize ourselves with our measures of rule, our jurisdictions and the laws of every place, kingdom or realm that we plan to enter.

Again, there are seven Mountains of Influence. These mountains are guarded by legalities or laws; they all have boundaries, penalties and allowances. The same is true for every side of each mountain and every range of each mountain. If you break a law, you could end up dead or imprisoned. For example, the Mountain of Religion is divided into 4,200 sections, and in each of these sections, lies a kingdom. In each of these sections, you'll find a religion and the people who support that religion. There is the kingdom of Christianity and there is a kingdom of Islam. In order for us to venture into one of the Islamic kingdoms, we would have to honor the laws of that kingdom or, as some people say, "When in Rome, do as the Romans do!" In other words, don't stand out! Some years ago, it was illegal for women in Saudi Arabia or Iran to leave their homes without wearing a hijab and an abaya. Foreign women who visited these countries had to abide by these strict laws. While these laws have been lifted, the residue of those beliefs are still so strong that in 2018, 29 women were arrested for removing their hijabs in public during a protest in Saudi Arabia. Howbeit, there are laws present in every country that aren't necessarily present elsewhere, so when you visit those countries, you must abide by their laws or, at minimum, honor their customs.
As we discussed in the previous section, mountains are divided into sections called altitudinal

zones. These zones are guarded by laws (restrictions, allowances), edges (boundaries) and penalties (consequences). If you were ascending a natural mountain, you'd respect the law of gravity while climbing the mountain. You wouldn't jump off the mountain or attempt to skip the steps needed to get to each level. The same is true when venturing up or down one of the Mountains of Influence. You can't just jump to another level; you have to ascend one step at a time. And just like Adam and Eve fell dimensionally when they'd sinned, you must ascend dimensionally; this means that ascension has everything to do with your mindset, and not your decisions! Now, your decisions are the fruit of your mindset, so it's easy to understand why so many people are law-minded! When ascending the Mountain of Family, for example, you have to follow God's Word. So, if you're unmarried, the Word of God dictates that you refrain from premarital sex. But just like all mountains, there is a very present temptation that men and women face while courting; this temptation is to skip a few steps while rushing toward what they believe to be the peak. But just like Abraham, any time you come to a new place, any time you're faced with temptation, you have to build an altar and you have to put your flesh and your will on that altar! If you skip a step, you will destabilize what otherwise could have been a stable relationship! This is what we call protocols and processes. Immature believers don't respect protocol, nor are they patient enough to endure the processes, seasons and sacrifices needed to ascend. This is why it is commonplace today to see aspiring leaders attacking established leaders on social media. This is no different than what non-kings used to do in the biblical era; many men who aspired to become kings themselves would conspire to kill their own king or the king of another nation. The goal was to overthrow the king and usurp his authority. This is what Absalom conspired to do to his own father. And in attempting this, he broke a sleuth of laws, which resulted in his untimely death. This is why the scriptures tell us to be anxious for nothing! This is why the scriptures tell us that long-suffering is a fruit of the Spirit! Another word for long-suffering is patience, and patience is needed to ascend any of the Mountains of Influence! Leaders who lack patience have to remain at the bottom of these mountains and eat whatever grows at the base of the mountains that they are called to! This is why so many creatives complain about not being able to find a job; the problem isn't spiritual, it's practical! The simple answer is the creative has not yet consumed and properly digested the fruits needed to sustain him or her at the base level! Like a baby, the creative keeps vomiting up the experiences, instead of taking the nutrients from each encounter. This means that the prophet or prophetic model would not be able to survive on another level or range of the mountain, so God's mercy keeps the creative from being promoted. This is why every prophet needs a mentor; this is why every prophetic model needs a therapist!

Let's revisit the topic of altitudinal zonation. We talked about the different zones of a mountain and how they affect vegetation. Look at the chart below to see what grows at each level.

Range	Vegetation
15,000 Feet (Snow Line)	Peak, Frozen
12,000 Feet (Tree Line)	Animals Graze
6,000 Feet	Barley, Potatoes
2,500 Feet	Apples, Grapes, Corn, Coffee, Small Grains
Sea Level	Bananas, Sugarcane, Rice

Galatians 5:22-23 reads, "But the fruit of the Spirit is love, joy, peace, patience, kindness, goodness, faithfulness, gentleness, self-control; against such things there is no law." Just like every level or zone of a mountain encourages the development of certain fruit, every phase of your life and your ministry will require certain fruit. The fruit of the Spirit will develop as you allow God to terraform your mind and transform your perspective. If you don't have teeth to chew bananas, God's definitely not going to give you an apple! If you keep vomiting up or, better yet, complaining about your experiences at 2,500 feet, why would God permit you to ascend to the next level? Think about it! When you learn to respect the zone and the laws of the level that you're on, promotion is inevitable! When you learn to take the nutrients from every experience and encounter, both negative and positive, promotion is inevitable!

The Influencer Model

Influencers are social media personalities that have built a small to large following; these leaders have specialized knowledge in a specific area. With the rise of social media, it is common to see people rushing towards the many peaks of success. There's a problem with this model and that is, a large number of these people have no pastors; they are not submitted to anyone! This means that many of them are stars who don't have an Elijah to guide them. To the average person, this may seem harmless enough, but the problem with this is, every level of a mountain requires specialized gear. On the Mountain of Religion, we call this gear a mantle. One of the purposes of a mantle was to keep the person wearing it warm, all the while, concealing the person's humanity. It kept the wearer warm, it kept the wearer humble and it protected the wearer from other external threats like insects and thorns. When a father passed his mantle to his son, he transported or transferred his experiences, but not the pain or the pressure that came with those encounters. This allowed the son to ascend the same mountains without having to create his own mantle along the way. In other words, this allowed the son to ascend the mountain must faster than his father had. But many of the influencers you see today don't have a mantle! Remember, in every zone, the temperature is different, the vegetation is different, the animals are different and the pressures are different. As you ascend a mountain, the temperatures drop more, making it colder and windier towards the top. The

wind represents words; these words come in the form of:
- doctrines
- opinions
- witchcraft

Most Westerners would argue that they aren't bothered by the opinions of man and they aren't moved by the demonic doctrines, but if you pay close attention, you'll notice a trend. Many influencers who aren't accountable to anyone start flirting with New Age beliefs once they reach the wind chills of 100 thousand followers or more. They start promoting pagan doctrines and attempting to mix them with Christian beliefs. The reason for this is, New Age beliefs are a growing trend, so a large number of their followers are new agers! The influencer begins to depend on getting a certain number of views, a certain number of sales and a certain amount of ads. Whenever their numbers begin to dwindle, they look for ways to get their numbers back up, so they'll look at other influencers. Noticing that some of the influencers that they follow are growing in their influence, they start monitoring their posts and their comments. Realizing that they are pro everything that God is against, the influencer begins to reason within himself or herself that maybe the church has it wrong after all!; they start reasoning that maybe the church is ignorant and maybe they need to open up their minds to new doctrines when the Bible told us to guard our hearts! So, the influencer bites into the forbidden fruit and is immediately intoxicated by fame, intoxicated by pride and intoxicated by rebellion. Not realizing that the influencer is now under the influence of demonic doctrines, most of the influencer's followers keep following him or her and eating whatever it is that the influencer is feeding them! This causes the sheep to become intoxicated; they then begin to wander away from their churches because their diets have been altered. They wander into the enemy's territories where they find Satan, as a roaring lion, going about seeking someone to devour.

Followers/Vegetation	Influencer Type
1M+	Mega, Celebrity
100K-1M	Macro
20K-100K	Mid Tier
5K-20K	Micro
1K-5K	Nano

Every follower represents a wind chill. Many of the followers have a specialized diet that has been crafted for them by their pastors. Of course, I'm not saying that people should stop following social media influencers, after all, many of them are doctrinally sound and they are accountable with what they teach! What I am saying is, believers should always do as the Bible says and test the spirit. If the influencer is influencing people, especially on the Mountain of Religion, and that influencer doesn't have a pastor, that influencer is under the influence! In other words, don't follow people who refuse to follow people! And as a prophet or prophetic model, your job isn't to rush towards the top, your job is to eat what's on the level that you're on. Digest it and grow. As you mature and develop, your influence will increase. Don't allow the enemy to tempt you with ambition; this is why, as a pastor, I am leery about sheep who are in a rush to become shepherds or sheep that chase after mics and platforms. This is usually a sign of immaturity; this is why Jesus had to leave the 99 to go after the one that wandered off. Get this—sheep have a strong instinctual need to follow one another! If a sheep or an influencer wanders off into demonic doctrines, a large number of their followers will start flirting with those doctrines as well!

As you ascend, remember that every level has pressure and you need to be properly clothed for every level that you ascend you. You need a mantle! Sure, you can create your own , but this normally takes a lifetime to accomplish! Remember this formula:
1. For every mountain, there is a mantle.
2. For every mantle, there is a measure.
3. For every measure, there is a moment.

Ecclesiastes 3:1 says it this way, "To every thing there is a season, and a time to every purpose under the heaven." In other words, eat according to the level that you're on and the season that you're in. When you see influencers rushing past you without a pastor, don't chase after them. Just keep eating! The law of gravity suggests that those same people who ran up the mountain will eventually roll down it.

Attitudinal Zonation

Every mountain has a dress code. and every mountain has laws that govern it. For example, you wouldn't wear the same outfit to church that you wore to a concert. Every outfit or uniform has its own place. All the same, each level of the mountain requires that you layer yourself all the more. Your outfit represents your attitude or how you respond to the many vicissitudes of life and people.

You may feel called to the top of one of the seven mountains, and more than likely, what you're sensing is truly the call of God on your life. Most of us have a call on our lives; this is why the scripture says that many are called, but few are chosen. You pass by "called" people every day, and the reason they are not necessarily chosen is because they don't want to be used by God or they refuse to let God transform their minds. So, the "chosen" ones aren't a special group of X-Men that have supernatural powers and abilities; they are people who said "yes" to the call on their lives. These are the people who put their hands to the plow and refused to let go or to look back. Sadly enough, not everyone who puts their hands on the assignment remains committed to their calls. This has everything to do with their attitudes.

Your attitude is the position of your heart; it is the weather of your personality. While we, as humans, are complex creatures, our makeup is very similar to the makeup of the planet. Because we are multidimensional creatures, we have many different branches of us, all of which are similar to countries, and all of those zones have states. For example, you are a world, and inside of you, there are seven Mountains of Influence. You have:

1. **Your religious identity:** This has everything to do with your religious affiliations, your religious beliefs and your relationship with God.
2. **Your familial identity:** This is how you identify yourself based on your family structure; this is also is reflected in your relationship with your family and your attitude towards families.
3. **Your political identity:** This is your government identity; this deals with your political affiliations and your political beliefs.
4. **Your educational identity:** This encompasses how you feel and relate to knowledge, and this is often expressed in your passion or nonchalant attitude towards the educational system in your country.
5. **Your entrepreneurial identity:** This deals with your ability to create wealth through problem-solving. It also deals with your financial disciplines.
6. **Your medial identity:** This details how you deal with the world and everything that's happening in it. Are you concerned about world hunger? Do you know what's going on both locally and abroad? What are you doing to change the world?
7. **Your entertainment identity:** This is where a lot of your time and money is invested. What you are entertained by is a reflection of what you're either called to or bound by.

Every one of these zones have states or conditions. You may be a sound, mature and faithful Christian, but your financial man may be immature and unstable. You may be extremely educated in one area, but completely ignorant in another. Where you have the most knowledge, you'll often have the most passion. But knowledge without understanding is the formula for pride; this is why the scripture tells us, "In all thy getting, get understanding." Understanding is the gravity that keeps a man grounded when knowledge begins to puff him up. Wherever you lack knowledge is normally the area where you'll display the most instability, both emotionally and financially. But when all of these areas are filled with knowledge, grounded by understanding and submitted to God, the man then becomes what the scriptures refer to as "whole." Luke detailed the account of ten lepers. Let's review the story. "And it came to pass, as he went to Jerusalem, that he passed through the midst of Samaria and Galilee. And as he entered into a certain village, there met him ten men that were lepers, which stood afar off: And they lifted up their voices, and said, Jesus, Master, have mercy on us. And when he saw them, he said unto them, Go shew yourselves unto the priests. And it came to pass, that, as they went, they were cleansed. And one of them, when he saw that he was healed, turned back, and with a loud voice glorified God, And fell down on his face at his feet, giving him thanks: and he was a Samaritan. And Jesus answering said, Were there not ten cleansed?" (Luke 17:11-17).

In this story, we meet ten men who all had leprosy. They all approached Jesus and the first thing that they did was acknowledge Him as Master. They then asked for mercy; in other words, they asked to be healed of their ailment. Jesus had compassion on them and told them to go and show themselves to the priests. Leprosy, in that era, was incurable. It was normally characterized by pale, white skin. The diseased person would oftentimes be covered with ulcers, large bumps and their skin would be scaly. They would look like something out of a horror film! The Law at that time required lepers to be declared unclean if the priest determined that their leprosy was dangerous. If a leper was declared unclean, he would be cast out of society. Leprosy was seen as a divine curse and divine punishment for either the sins of the person or the sins of the individual's parents. Again, the men asked for mercy; the Greek word for "mercy" is "eleos," which means compassion, so the men asked for compassion. Jesus had compassion on them and told them to go and show themselves to the priests. The priests could declare them clean again, which would allow them to reenter society. They obeyed Him, and as they journeyed toward the temple, they were all healed. This was another great miracle that Jesus performed. But of all the men, only one turned around and gave glory to the Lord. How did Jesus respond? First, He questioned the whereabouts of the other nine. This tells us that Jesus was disappointed in the men who had not turned back and glorified God, but He performed another miracle for the man who had honored Him. He said, "Arise and go your way. Your faith has made you whole." What Jesus did for this man was remarkable. He pretty much touched every area of His life; He touched every mountain in His life, thus, causing him to bear fruit. The million-dollar question is, why didn't the others turn around and glorify God? It's called entitlement. Entitlement is a leprosy of the mind; it's filthy, it's ugly, it's scaly and it deforms the character of the individual!

Most prophets and prophetic models (creatives) are not defeated by Jezebel; they are defeated by pride! Pride is the "great fish" that swallows the majority of the people who are called by God! This is why they are called, but not chosen! Pride is the graveyard for the living; it is a holding cell for death! Nine lepers walked away healed, but they were not made whole! The scripture even makes mention of the fact that the one who had turned back and given God the glory was a Samaritan. Samaritans were half-Jew, half-Gentile. The Samaritans came on the scene in 721 B.C. after the Assyrians captured the northern kingdom of Israel. Ten of the northern tribes separated from Judah, and eventually began to accept foreign doctrines and beliefs. These Israelites stayed behind and intermarried with the Assyrians. Their offspring are what the Bible refers to as Samaritans. The Samaritans eventually turned away from many of their idolatrous beliefs and adopted some parts of the Jewish religion. Nevertheless, they were rejected by the "pure" Jews, and like lepers, they were considered outcasts. But it was the Samaritan man who'd turned around and gave God the glory, whereas, the other men (presumably Jewish) were so religious, rejected and entitled that they didn't display any form of gratitude. A lack of gratitude is the result of a bad attitude and/or a wrong perspective! They were so determined to show themselves, not just to the priests, but to the folks who'd laughed at them, rejected them and the folks who'd said they deserved to be outcasts that they neglected to give, at minimum, their reasonable service. This is similar to what many believers do today, especially believers who've been saved for a long time. This is why we have to consistently check our attitudes! If you are not moving up the mountain that you're called to … if you're stuck at a certain altitude, be sure to check your attitude! You may not be a nasty human being, but the problem could be that somehow, along the journey, you picked up pride and entitlement, and now, your perspective has been severely deformed.

Maybe you feel like your pastor isn't promoting you fast enough, so you've decided to climb the mountain on your own; you've decided to build your own brand! Hear me—as a pastor, I see this all the time! And if I can be the voice of reason in your life, if I can be the voice of your pastor for a moment, let me share with you why your pastor may know that you're anointed, but still never call on you to preach, to teach or to pray. It's not that your pastor is trying to constrict you—it's not that you're in the wrong church! The problem is, as a pastor, we have to look at how you're handling the zone or season that you're in, and what is consistently being produced in your life. We also have to look at how you are emotionally handling the season that you're in. In other words, we have to examine your attitude. Your attitude produces your personal atmosphere; it is the scent of your personality! That atmosphere is going to attract people who have the same spirit as you or repel people who have a contrary spirit. In other words, the company you keep does matter! Think of it this way—if I was your pastor and you were at the base level of your calling, my job isn't to promote you, my job is to prepare you for promotion! So, if you can't handle correction, if you have problems with punctuality or if you are still struggling with your identity, I wouldn't be a great pastor if I promoted you, seeing that you are still being tossed to and fro by base-level winds! My job is to carefully construct a diet for you that allows you to grow and to stand firm on the level that you're on! When you're solid enough, when you're grounded enough and when you're mature enough, you'll eat your way up the mountain! All I have to do is prepare the menu, and then, pay attention to what you order from the menu! If you keep demanding my attention, asking for a mic or complaining about what you're not getting, you're still ordering from the kid's menu! Hear me—the amount of time it takes to grow you is completely up to you! You have to eat what I preach, you have to show up when I teach and you have to consume everything I make available! Next, you have to wrestle with the lions, the tigers and every one of the bears that come your way! And trust me, they're coming! These are the devils that no one sees you fighting! They can range in size from anger to the temptation to leave the church! If you can wrestle these beasts to the ground, if you can confront and overthrow your own personal Goliaths and if you can maintain your honor and your humility while doing all of these things, you'll soon discover that you don't need a mic because your life will become a mic! This is the mystery of ministry! Children are anxious to be seen, but all of creation is waiting eagerly for the revealing of the sons of God! Hear me—creation is not waiting on you to get a mic or a new camera, all of creation is waiting on you to realize who you are! When you eat everything that your pastor puts out for you, this is how you increase your weight; this is how you become a force within yourself that the winds can't move! If you're at church two Sundays out of the month, you're not ready for promotion! This isn't to punish you, it's to prepare you!

The people you surround yourself with are symbolic of the animals that come to each zone of a mountain to feast on the vegetation that grows there. I'm not calling your friends or loved ones animals, I'm just making a point! But if you're easily offended or surrounded by people who are highly emotional, chances are, you haven't been fully terraformed or, better yet, transformed by the renewing of your mind. Listen, this is okay! It's simply where you are right now, but my charge to you is just don't stay there! If you haven't been transformed, it goes without saying that you can't transform anyone else, nor can you transform any of the Mountains of Influence! The first person that you have to influence is the person you see every time you look in the mirror! Understand that every level on a mountain comes with a certain amount of pressure. When pressure manifests itself in humans, it manifests as depression, repression and suppression! These are the many pressings that form what we call pressure! It's what causes stars to collapse within themselves and to burnout prematurely. And if you don't properly manage yourself while you are going through the "pressing," you'll start oppressing others!

If the pressure from the level that you're on is too much for you, please don't try to rush up the mountain! And of course, you may ask, "How do I know if I'm managing my zone or my season properly?" Look at your attitude! The Bible says that God loves a *cheerful* giver! This scripture isn't just dealing with your money, it's dealing with your time and everything that has any weight or value (mass) in your life! If you get angry and stop praying because God didn't do what you wanted Him to do when you wanted Him to do it, you're not managing your season properly! This means that you don't have an attitude of gratitude, but instead, you are still dealing with an attitude of entitlement. Your attitude will determine what and who you attract into your life. People with bad attitudes typically surround themselves with others who are emotionally unstable. This is what I call attitudinal zonation.

Attitudinal zonation doesn't just apply to you and your personal ascension, but you should also apply this to your relationships and your ministry! For example, we all know not to mix bleach with ammonia or bleach with vinegar because they are chemically incompatible. When they come in contact with one another, they release dangerous gases and vapors. The way you position the people in your life is a reflection of your maturity! For example, if you have a friend who explodes with anger every time you have a heart-to-heart conversation with that friend, chances are, the two of you are incompatible. Proverbs 22:24-25 states, "Make no friendship with an angry man; and with a furious man thou shalt not go: Lest thou learn his ways, and get a snare to thy soul." This scripture isn't telling you to turn your nose up at angry or emotional people, it's literally dealing with intimacy. It's dealing with the proximity of your heart to that person's heart. Amos 3:3 asks the question, "Can two walk together except they be in agreement?" For example, many of us have been given the peg test as children. We were handed a plastic or wooden board that was full of holes. Each hole had a certain shape; one of the holes had a square shape, another had a round shape and another had a triangular shape. We were then handed a bunch of pegs—one of those pegs was square, one was round and the other was triangular. This test was done to see if we were developmentally healthy. Our teachers would stand by quietly and watch to see if we placed the round pegs in the round holes or if we tried to place them elsewhere. If we tried to fit pegs into holes that were not in the same shape that they were, our teachers knew to call our parents and give them the bad news. When observing the people on your leadership team or the people around you, pay attention to who they have in their lives and where those people are situated in their lives. You'll notice that some of the people who appear to be the smartest oftentimes lack relational intelligence. This is your own personal peg test; it shows that they are still sleeping on themselves; they are still unaware or ignorant of their own identities. This means that all of creation is still waiting on them to wake up! Again, this is okay! They aren't bad people; they're simply still in the wombs of their purpose! You don't promote, platform or partner up with people who have identity issues! You'll know that they have matured when they learn to put everyone in the right place! This is attitudinal zonation; it is a reflection of a person's maturity or immaturity.

Prophetic Activation

Today, you are an influencer! That's right! You're about to take your influence to social media! Record a short three to fifteen-minute video clip of you testifying about something God brought you through, and detail how that event changed you for the better. No bitter stories or attempts to humiliate other people! This is all about encouraging your viewers! This assignment may be uncomfortable, but you should see the benefits of it after a few days!

Mission Seven

T-03

Constellations

1 Samuel 10:9-11: And it was so, that when he had turned his back to go from Samuel, God gave him another heart: and all those signs came to pass that day. And when they came thither to the hill, behold, a company of prophets met him; and the Spirit of God came upon him, and he prophesied among them. And it came to pass, when all that knew him beforetime saw that, behold, he prophesied among the prophets, then the people said one to another, What is this that is come unto the son of Kish? Is Saul also among the prophets?

1 Samuel 19:19-24: And it was told Saul, saying, Behold, David is at Naioth in Ramah. And Saul sent messengers to take David: and when they saw the company of the prophets prophesying, and Samuel standing as appointed over them, the Spirit of God was upon the messengers of Saul, and they also prophesied. And when it was told Saul, he sent other messengers, and they prophesied likewise. And Saul sent messengers again the third time, and they prophesied also. Then went he also to Ramah, and came to a great well that is in Sechu: and he asked and said, Where are Samuel and David? And one said, Behold, they be at Naioth in Ramah. And he went thither to Naioth in Ramah: and the Spirit of God was upon him also, and he went on, and prophesied, until he came to Naioth in Ramah. And he stripped off his clothes also, and prophesied before Samuel in like manner, and lay down naked all that day and all that night. Wherefore they say, Is Saul also among the prophets?

Saul was a star. He was the king of Israel, so he was definitely a celebrity. In the aforementioned scriptures, we see two separate occasions of Saul prophesying. In 1 Samuel 10:9, Saul had not yet transgressed against the Lord, so it's no surprise to most believers that he found himself prophesying. But when we get to 1 Samuel 19, Saul had become a deeply disturbed, mentally unstable and prideful individual. His envy of David had grown into a murderous obsession with David; this made it difficult for him to focus on running the kingdom. So, David had gone on the run; he'd traveled to Ramah and told the Prophet Samuel everything that Saul had done to him, and the two men then took refuge in a place called Naioth, located in Ramah. The term Naioth has often been translated as "houses" or "habitations," but there is no biblical evidence to substantiate this. Naioth is believed to be a place where the prophets dwelt together; some theologians say that Saul had a school of prophets in Naioth. This would explain why Saul ran into a company of prophets there and why he too was overcome by the Spirit of the Lord. David was a rising star. And as God would have it, the two men's lives would align; this was so that David could be in position to assume his rightful role as the king of Israel.

Joseph was a star. Pharaoh was a star. They'd both come from two completely different worlds and constellations, but as God would have it, the two men would meet through a series of misfortunes, and Joseph would eventually become Pharaoh's right hand man. Get this—a series of lies positioned Joseph until he found himself in his God-given space. He found himself on top of the Mountain of Government, dressed like an Egyptian, but declaring the name of the Most High God. This is why God said, "If I be lifted up, I will draw all men unto me." How do we lift up the name of God? By climbing the mountains we're assigned to and promoting Him (no other deity) along the way.

Howbeit, before we go any further, let's look at a law called the Law of Proximity. It is one of the few Gestalt principles. The Law of Proximity deals with how we, as humans, perceive connections between visual elements. We normally perceive elements that are in close proximity as a single unit, but we mentally separate things that appear to be disconnected or far away from one another. Conversely, a lack of proximity implies a lack of relationship between two or more elements. The closer elements are together, the more likely we are to group them. Take a look at the dots below.

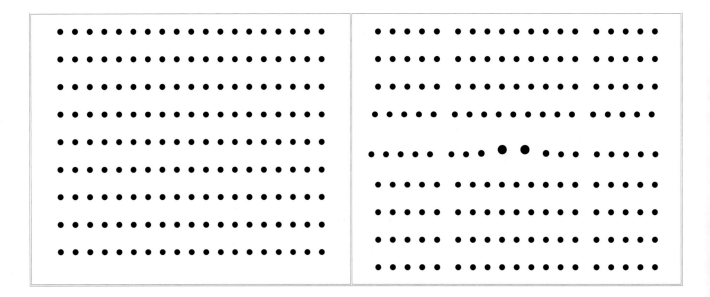

On the left, you see what appears to be a single square. Your eyes will identify the object on the left as related or as a unit, even though you see many dots. Howbeit, your eyes will likely perceive the object on the right as individual concepts or shapes. Notice that in the center of the elements on the right, two of the dots are significantly larger than the rest, nevertheless, your brain still groups them together.

Have you ever met a man or a woman who was just downright unpleasant? Maybe, you worked with the individual, went to school with the individual or the two of you attended the same church. One day, you noticed that the person had a certain group of people that he hung around, and for whatever reason, you found yourself seeing his friends the same way you saw him. Because of this, you struggled to communicate with his friends. You likely spoke to them or nodded your head at them, before retreating to "your group." This is the Gestalt principle in full effect. This, of course, answers the age-old question that many people seem to be plagued with, and that is, "Why haven't I been promoted on my job?" or "Why are there so many cliques at my church?" While I am not a fan of disunity, nor do I encourage it, I've come to understand that people pair or partner up with others who are like-minded. This gives weight to the age-old adage which states, "Birds of a feather, flock together!" This doesn't stop them from being birds, but it does help scientists to distinguish them! It definitely helped Adam to identify them and categorize them, even though they were all birds!

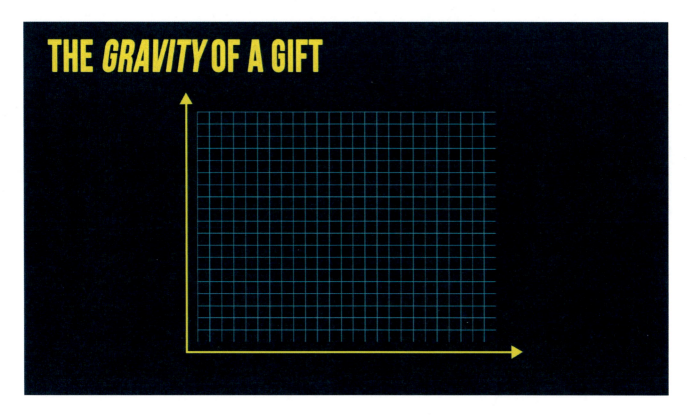

Another interesting Gestalt principle is the Law of Symmetry; it states that items that are symmetrical to one another tend to be perceived as related to one another. I like to think of it this way—your friends and your enemies are a prophecy of where you're headed! Elijah was a picture of where Elisha was going! Saul was a picture of where David was headed! And while they were not necessarily symmetrical in their influence whenever they climaxed in their assignments, both Elijah and Saul paved the way for their predecessors. Elijah paved a path for Elisha through honor; Saul unwittingly paved the way for David through his dishonor.

As a prophet or prophetic model, the company that you keep is important. Again, it determines how people see you, how fast doors or opportunities open and just how fast opportunities or doors shut for you. Think of it as a constellation. Now, before I define this word or delve deeper into this presentation, let me go ahead and dispel the belief that discussions about constellations or anything related to astronomy are all ungodly. Science, according to Google is "the intellectual and practical activity encompassing the systematic study of the structure and behavior of the physical and natural world through observation and experiment." Science deals with the natural world; witchcraft deals with the spirit world and how it affects or manipulates the natural world. In other words, astronomy is not New Age, nor is it occultist, however, people who promote and ascribe to New Age philosophies use astronomy and especially astrology to support, craft and promote their beliefs. Because of this, the church, at large, has been divorcing so many aspects of science and math; this has resulted in many believers becoming less educated and more emotional. And while the world has been educating its own and proving their points using scientific testing and data, we've been running around our prospective churches, screaming at the top of our lungs and dancing uncontrollably. Yes, run and praise God; this is all great and good, but you should also be filling your head with knowledge! In Hosea 4:6, God says, "My people are destroyed for lack of knowledge: because thou hast rejected knowledge, I will also reject thee, that thou shalt be no priest to me: seeing thou hast forgotten the law of thy God, I will also forget thy children." Of course, theologians and intellectuals alike could debate about this, but this scripture isn't just dealing with spiritual knowledge or biblical knowledge, it is also dealing with natural knowledge; it is dealing with every law that God has instituted in the Earth realm and the spirit realm. The word "knowledge" encompasses what we know. There are many realms of knowledge in both the natural world and the spiritual world, and we don't necessarily need or ascribe to some of it, we should be cramming our heads with as much knowledge as we can! But we've become so religious and afraid of knowledge that we often lose souls because we keep trying to counter their practicality with spirituality. Apostle Paul said it this way, "But the natural man receiveth not the things of the Spirit of God: for they are foolishness unto him: neither can he know them, because they are spiritually discerned" (1 Corinthians 2:14). I say that to say, we can't keep rejecting everything that the occult starts embracing; they can explain it to their people one way, but we can teach it to the church through the filter of truth. Facts that are filtered by truth birth revelation. Note: I'm not telling you to go out and look up information that you don't necessarily have the teeth to chew; don't start looking too deep into astronomy if you don't have a pastor or someone who can help guide you in that world. I say that because the gulf or the membrane between the world of astronomy and the world of astrology is so remarkably thin that you can easily venture off into New Age philosophies, and if you're not properly mantled, you could easily pick up the scent of that world. This is why I am for having a pastor and being accountable. Your pastor knows how mature you are and whether you need to layer yourself with more biblical information before you start snooping around in other regions or religions.

What is a constellation? Google defines it this way, "A group of stars forming a recognizable pattern that is traditionally named after its apparent form or identified with a mythological figure. Modern astronomers divide the sky into eighty-eight constellations with defined boundaries."

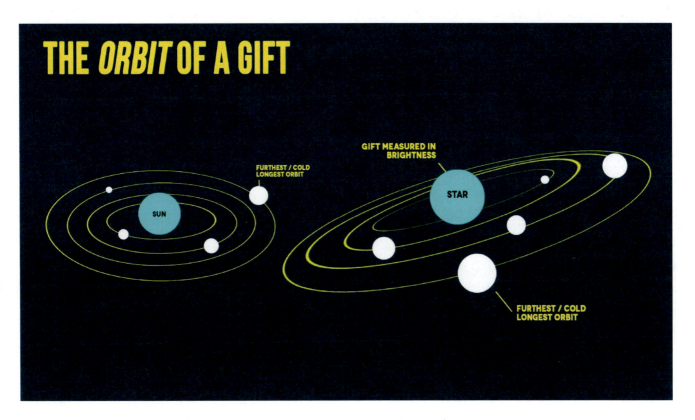

The truth is, a constellation is just an imaginary star pattern; scientists have basically linked several groups of stars together, even though they aren't necessarily close to one another or related. Just so you know, there are different groupings of stars. They include:
- **Binary stars:** A binary star is a star system consisting of two stars orbiting around their common barycenter (Wikipedia).
- **Open clusters:** An open cluster is a group of up to a few thousand stars that were formed from the same giant molecular cloud and have roughly the same age (Wikipedia).
- **Global clusters:** A globular cluster is a spherical collection of stars that orbits a galactic core. Globular clusters are very tightly bound by gravity, which gives them their spherical shapes, and relatively high stellar densities toward their centers (Wikipedia).
- **Galaxies:** A galaxy is a gravitationally bound system of stars, stellar remnants, interstellar gas, dust, and dark matter (Wikipedia).
- **Constellations:** A constellation is an area on the celestial sphere in which a group of

stars forms an imaginary outline or pattern, typically representing an animal, mythological person or creature, or an inanimate object (Wikipedia).
- **Asterism:** In observational astronomy, an asterism is a popularly known pattern or group of stars that can be seen in the night sky. This colloquial definition makes it appear quite similar to a constellation, but they differ mostly in that a constellation is an officially recognized area of the sky, while an asterism is a visually obvious collection of stars and the lines used to mentally connect them; as such, asterisms do not have officially determined boundaries and are therefore a more general concept which may refer to any identified pattern of stars (Wikipedia).

When Joseph was a young man, he was favored by his father, Jacob. Howbeit, he was hated by his brothers. Of course, we know that his brothers would eventually plot his death, but would settle on the idea of selling him into slavery simply because of a chanced encounter. Joseph would then be taken to Egypt and sold by the Midianites to one of Pharaoh's officials by the name of Potiphar; the Bible says that Potiphar was the captain of Pharaoh's guard. This means that he was a very important official in Egypt. Some translations of the Bible suggest (but do not assert) that Potiphar may have been a eunuch, but there is no evidence to support this. Eunuchs rarely married, but in some rare cases, they did. As the story goes, Potiphar's wife would make one last attempt to lay with Joseph, but his rejection of her would send her over the edge. In one of the worst cases of fatal attraction to date, Mrs. Potiphar would lie to her husband and anyone who would listen, saying that Joseph had attempted to rape her. Consequently, Potiphar would throw Joseph in prison, where he would sit for at least two years. What was happening here? The stars were aligning. Of course, I'm not talking about the stars in the sky, I'm talking about Joseph and Pharaoh. Joseph had a date with destiny, but the underground railroad used to get him to his promised land was through the wombs of hardship and betrayal. The same was true for a young queen-to-be named Esther. She would lose her parents at a young age and be raised by her cousin, Mordecai. Before she'd become queen, Esther lived in exile along with Mordecai. Even though the Jews had been freed and given permission to return to Jerusalem, many of them had stayed behind. Life, for Esther, had been abnormal. Nevertheless, the young star would eventually find herself partnering with another star (King Ahasuerus, also known as King Xerxes), and because of her obedience and submission, she would save the remaining Jews from Haman's genocidal fantasies. Again, two stars aligned from two completely different worlds so that the will of God could be carried out. These events were both supernaturally designed to protect and save the Jews. Of course, in Joseph's case, some years later, the Jews would be taken into captivity in Egypt when a new Pharaoh rose to power, but during his time or tenure, Joseph's assignment was to open the door for his family, who lived in Canaan so that they would not be affected by the oncoming famine. Joseph said to his brothers, "I am your brother Joseph, whom you sold into Egypt.

Now do not be grieved or angry with yourselves, because you sold me here, for God sent me before you to preserve life. For the famine has been in the land these two years, and there are still five years in which there will be neither plowing nor harvesting. God sent me before you to preserve for you a remnant in the earth, and to keep you alive by a great deliverance. Now, therefore, it was not you who sent me here, but God; and He has made me a father to Pharaoh and lord of all his household and ruler over all the land of Egypt" (Genesis 45:4–8). The reason I shared those two stories is to show you the strategic and intentional nature of God. You are a star.

The seven mountains all represent worlds. These worlds are divided into kingdoms. Every kingdom has a womb; this is the door in which we enter through. Many of us have been birthed out into these worlds through the wombs of hurt, rejection and betrayal. However, the mistake that many creatives make is that we don't always remove the afterbirth; this is the residue of our pain, the puss that permeates our perspectives and the dirt underneath our purposes; this is the dust that God told us to shake from beneath our feet as a testimony against our enemies! Howbeit, we've tracked the dust from our former worlds into our new worlds, creating a path for our past (and every devil in it) to follow us. And when the devils that we got delivered from came looking for us, they were able to follow the trails made from our footsteps, and while they found our houses (temples) swept and garnished, they also found us sweeping around other folks' doorsteps, instead of our own. So, we ended up in a different world or on a different level, bound and weighed down by the same spirits that we once took into captivity. The weight caused us to collapse within ourselves, and we discovered that, like the earth realm, the spirit realm has its own version of gravity; it's called humility. Either we could humble ourselves and get free for real or we could follow blind leaders into ditches, where we'd spend the rest of our lives in the pits of religion and repetition. However, if we allowed the water of the Word to wash away the afterbirth, if we allowed God to pull the revelation out of our experiences, we would find that our pain served as the gravitational pull between us and our purposes.

Again, humility is the gravity of the spiritual world. Those who are humble in heart submit to the laws of humility, while those who are proud are brought down. 1 Peter 5:6 states, "Humble yourselves, therefore, under God's mighty hand, that he may lift you up in due time." In short, what this scripture is saying is that God will cause you to defy gravity so that He can take you up the Mountain of Influence that you're called to ascend. And get this—humility is the force that draws the right people into your life; these are the stars that you are called to eventually align yourself with. These are the men and women in seats of authority who God has graced to favor you. Proverbs 16:18 says, "A man's gift maketh room for him, and bringeth him before great men." Most men and women are gifted; most men and women are talented, so why is it that our graveyards are filled with gifted folks who never went before great and powerful men and women? Earlier we discussed being a creative versus being creative. The same is true for gifting. Everyone on the face of this planet is gifted (adjective), but not everyone is a gift (noun). The difference between the two is called investment (action and energy). When a person who is gifted decides to become a blessing, that person then becomes a gift. When you operate as a gift, you start attracting other gifts into your life. This is because the gravitational pull between humble and gifted souls is a strong and stable magnetic force. Think of it this way—gravity causes Earth and every other planet in our solar system to orbit the sun; this is why they are grouped together as a part of our solar system.

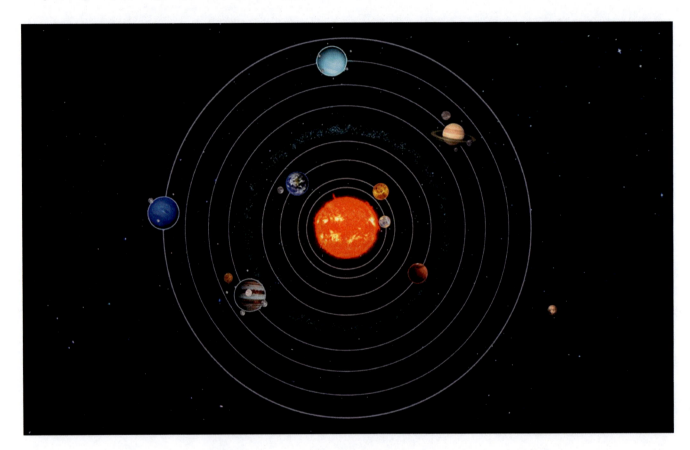

The phrase "solar system" describes the relationship that all of these planets and their moons have with the sun. The sun is what links us all together. Isn't it remarkable how the Son of God links us together with the people who make their debuts in our lives? What's even more remarkable is that, in our solar system, there are asteroids which, of course, serve as a danger to our planet and our moon. As a matter of fact, both the Earth and the moon have suffered innumerable attacks from asteroids, however, neither our planet nor our moon has succumbed to those attacks. We can see the evidence of the impacts on the moon because of the moon's many craters.

The moon cannot heal itself because it has no atmosphere, but the Earth managed to absorb the attacks because we do have an atmosphere, and most of what enters the Earth from outer space is destroyed the minute it enters our atmosphere. Between

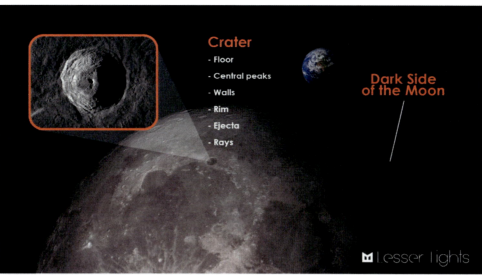

two hundred to four hundred objects enter the Earth's atmosphere a year, but most of them disintegrate upon entry. Any objects that do not disintegrate normally falls into one of our oceans. Oceans cover 71 percent of the Earth's surface!

Again, the Son of God links us all together, but before we can find the people in our constellation or the creatives who have been chosen to link our purposes with their purposes, we have to submit to the law of humility. There was a gravitational force pulling David and Jonathan together; this was done so that David would receive the impartation of knowledge that he would need to serve as the future king of Israel. There was a gravitational force that drew King Xerxes to Esther; he couldn't explain his attraction to the young beauty, but all he knew was that there was something about her that made him want to align his name with her name. There was an undeniable force that pulled Moses into Pharaoh's castle, allowing him to be raised by the king that he was appointed to defeat! There was a gravitational pull between Daniel and King Nebuchadnezzar II that caused the king to give him favor. As you can see, some of the most influential people in the Bible found themselves in the castles of idolatrous kings; they found themselves on one of the Mountains of Influence in pagan kingdoms serving the Most High God. This is why you can't be religious or intimidated by the world and their leaders. There are prophets and prophetic models planted in every world, just as there are tares in our world. God plants His people in questionable places, but then, notice that He surrounds them with prophetic companies. King Xerxes slowly but surely saw his courts changing. Haman was hung and Mordecai, Esther's cousin, took his place. Pharaoh had Joseph serving as his prophet, advisor and right-hand man. Daniel served both King Nebuchadnezzar and his son King Belshazzar. Daniel 2:48-49 reads, "Then the king promoted Daniel and gave him many generous gifts. He made him ruler over the entire province of Babylon and chief administrator over all the wise men of Babylon. And at Daniel's request, the king appointed Shadrach, Meshach, and Abednego to manage the province of Babylon, while

Daniel remained in the king's court." These men served as Daniel's prophetic company.

Who you surround yourself with will either pull you towards your purpose or away from it. Sometimes, to get you into position, God has to allow your constellations or asterim (relationships and associations) to break apart. In other cases, He allows the pain and the pressure behind the pain to reposition you. To push you into place or to pull you out of the networks that you've settled yourself in, God sometimes will destroy or interrupt the gravitons that encourage you to walk together with the people you're in agreement with; He does this by confusing your languages. This is what He did when the people of the Earth tried to build a tower to Heaven (the Tower of Babel). When God confused their language, He simply made it impossible for them to communicate with one another or understand one another. Sometimes, there are people who've been in our lives for years (decades even) who speak English, but they suddenly stopped speaking our language. To do this, all God has to do was to change what we were attracted to. Amos 3:3 asks the question, "Can two walk together except they be agreed?" All of the planets and moons in our solar system are attracted to the sun; if one of them were to lose their attraction to the sun, it would leave our solar system. This would cause it to abandon or break away from the other planets in our solar system as well. The same is true for us.

Constellations

All too often, the people who are in our lives are centered around or drawn to the same things or the same people that we are drawn to. This is what we call agreement. To end this agreement, God will often change what we center ourselves around or vice versa. This causes us to venture further and further away from one another until there is no force or agreement pulling or linking us together. After we remove the residue from our old worlds and our old experiences, we start attracting the stars who are designed to serve alongside us. This is our prophetic company; these people are the forces and the fuel that we need to ascend into our seats of authority.

Like most prophets and creatives, you may have experienced an astronomical amount of hardships in your life. But if I can use science to describe what you've experienced, are experiencing or will experience, I would explain it this way …

1. You are a star, but a young star in development is called a protostar. We all start off as protostars. A protostar is a star in its earliest stage of evolution.
2. Stars form in relatively small clouds called dense cores. In the western world, we often use the word "dense" when referencing people who some say are "not so bright," meaning, they lack revelation. A large number of prophets and prophetic models were developed in dark spaces. In other words, their families or communities were their first training grounds!
3. Every new star goes through nucleosynthesis. According to Wikipedia, "Stellar nucleosynthesis is the creation (nucleosynthesis) of chemical elements by nuclear fusion reactions within stars." But get this, stars go through fission before they go through fusion. What's the difference? According to Energy.gov, "Fission occurs when a neutron slams into a larger atom, forcing it to excite and split into two smaller atoms—also known as fission products." The site goes on to say that, "Fusion occurs when two atoms slam together to form a heavier atom, like when two hydrogen atoms fuse to form one helium atom." Hear me—before God brings the gift (you) into the presence of great men, He stores a certain amount of energy in your core; this energy is called potential. To provoke the release of your potential, God will often allow you to collide with an opposing force that is equal to or greater than the size of your calling! The reason for this is explained by Newton's Third Law of Motion, which states, "When one body exerts a force on a second body, the second body simultaneously exerts a force equal in magnitude and opposite in direction on the first body." In other words, the force behind the rejection, the force behind the betrayal and the force or power behind the lies pushed you into your purpose; they pushed you into position! But the fission or split that happened as a result of this collision is what we refer to as a "break up" or a "split up." These are the hardships brought on by watching the people we love and trust the most walk out of our lives. Howbeit, these "splits" are designed to propel us towards our

purpose and to align us with the right people. When we begin to merge with the right people, the energy in our core is released, and what was once potential becomes actualized power. Once we merge, we begin to emerge! This is why you shouldn't spend too much time grieving over folks who walked out of your life!

4. Once you connect with the right people, the real process of evolution begins. Slowly, you begin to develop until you not only reach your fullest potential, but you become your fullest potential. In other words, you become potent. God then uses the people you're connected to as a conduit to attract more people; this is how your constellation is formed! These are the people you are called to and these are the people who are called to you! Sure, you'll offend them and they'll offend you at some point, but let me explain to you what's happening when this takes place. Proverbs 27:17 reads, "Iron sharpens iron, and one man sharpens another." When two iron blades meet, they inadvertently sharpen one another; they also produce sparks or, better yet, power. This sharpening makes the blades more effective in their tasks and in warfare! Conversely, Ecclesiastes 10:10 says, "If the axe is dull and he does not sharpen its edge, then he must exert more strength. Wisdom has the advantage of giving success." In other words, without these experiences, a greater amount of energy, force or pain would be needed to extract the potential from your core! Sure, the betrayal hurt and yes, the rejection left a dent in your heart, but just like the craters on the moon, every dent is helping to craft the fingerprint that you will someday leave on the world that you're called to!

1 Corinthians 15:33 is a stark reminder for us all; it reads, "Be not deceived: evil communications corrupt good manners." In every world that you enter, on every mountain that you find yourself on and in every setting that you find yourself in, you will be judged by the company you keep. This may seem to be unfair to anyone who's surrounded by people with questionable character, but this is good news for everyone who surrounds themselves with people who have ascended and are ascending spiritually, morally, emotionally and maybe even academically. Every person in your life and every person who affects your movements in any way is a part of your ecosystem. Encyclopedia Britannica defines the word "ecosystem" this way: "the complex of living organisms, their physical environment, and all their interrelationships in a particular unit of space." The prefix "eco" literally means your environment, habitat or surroundings. Of course, your ecosystem deals with not just the company you keep, but every world, every language and everything you immerse yourself in. When all of these elements come together, they react and form what you call your reality. They set the stage for your victories and your losses. All the same, God often allows hardships, misunderstandings and chaotic events to cast us out of the company we keep. This is to ensure that everything He has invested in us does not go to waste.

If you want to prophesy more, hang around prophetic people and be sure to attend some of the prophetic activations that take place at your church or, at minimum, in your region. If you want to grow your creativity, hang around creatives, especially the ones who've activated their gifts and submitted them to their local assemblies.

Prophetic Activation

Today, find a prophetic activation event going on in your area and sign up for it! The event may be taking place three months from today, but either way, your assignment is to register for the event! If you can't find a prophetic activation taking place in your area anytime soon, call up at least three people and prophesy to them (if the Lord gives you something). Excuses are rooted in fear and insecurity! In other words, there is no room for them in your life or in this activation!

Mission Eight

T-02

Voice Commands

Term	Definition	Source
Sound Wave	longitudinal pressure waves in any material medium regardless of whether they constitute audible sound	Merriam Webster
Sound	mechanical radiant energy that is transmitted by longitudinal pressure waves in a material medium (such as air) and is the objective cause of hearing.	Merriam Webster
Voice	sound produced by vertebrates by means of lungs, larynx, or syrinx.	Merriam Webster
Frequency	in physics, the number of waves that pass a fixed point in unit time; also, the number of cycles or vibrations undergone during one unit of time by a body in periodic motion. A body in periodic motion is said to have undergone one cycle or one vibration after passing through a series of events or positions and returning to its original state.	Encyclopedia Britannica
Pitch	the quality of a sound governed by the rate of vibrations producing it; the degree of highness or lowness of a tone.	Google's Online Dictionary

Let's establish this fact first—there is no sound in space. Here's why. Sound is the energy produced by objects whenever they vibrate. If you punch a wall, the wall will begin to vibrate, forcing the air around it to also vibrate. These vibrations form sound waves; they travel through the air as the energy from the punch travels through the air. When it reaches your eardrums, it causes your eardrums to vibrate. Your eardrums respond by transmitting the information to your brain in the same pattern that the energy was received; your brain perceives the vibrations as sound. Sound waves travel through a medium (object) by causing atoms and molecules to vibrate back and forth. This means that in order for sound to be produced, it has to have an object to bounce off. Again, this object is called a medium. In space, there is a great amount of distance between stars, planets and moons, and because of this, sound has no medium to travel through and no one to travel to.

You are a medium. As we discovered earlier, a medium isn't necessarily an occultic word.

Sure, it's being used by the occult, and they are using it in the right context, however, the word "medium" simply means a "go-between." A witch or a warlock is a medium because they serve as connectors between fallen angels and people. A prophet or creative is a medium because they serve as a connector between God and His people. And get this—every medium serves as a transmitter. You transmit what God is saying through words, dance, song, drawing, painting, writing or whatever your creative expression may be.

Why did I start off this chapter saying that there is no sound in space? The simple answer is, there is no need for sound in space. Space was not created to be a domain for mankind, even though we have dreamed of living on the moon and possibly even living on other planets. In space, there is no one to talk to, so there was no reason for God to create sound outside of the Earth's realm. As a prophet or creative, you have a prophetic expression that God gave to you to communicate His will to others. You weren't created in a vacuum; you were born on a planet that has the benefits of sound. What this means is that you weren't created to be quiet; you were created to make noise. Most prophetic models are aware of this. But the question that often arises is, "When should I share my gift with the world?" and "What should I do if my pastor is not creating space for me to share my gift?" Let's start with the first question, but to answer this question, we have to delve into a little history.

Have you ever heard the word "castrati"? A castrati was a male singer who had been castrated before puberty so that he could retain his soprano or contralto voice. This practice dates back to 400 AD. but was popularized in the mid-17^h century in Italy. Castratos were very popular in European operas, churches and courts, even though the practice hadn't necessarily been legalized. Families would pay surgeons under the table to castrate their musically inclined sons because castratos brought in a lot of money. They were especially popular in operas. Of course, this was a practice done on a select number of male singers, mainly the ones who had very unique, high pitched voices. The boys were castrated to keep them from undergoing puberty which, of course, would significantly alter their voices. Castration prevented the production of testosterone, thus, allowing the young men to retain their youthful pitches, however, there had been some side effects—obviously! Without testosterone, their bones could not harden; this caused them to grow to become very tall men. Castratos had long bones and prominent rib cages. Of course, this only enhanced their voices. These men could hold a note for an unusual length of time, and they wowed audiences with their amazingly high pitches. In 1861, castration for musical purposes was officially called a crime, meaning, it was finally banned and labeled as a criminal act. In 1878, Pope Leo XIII prohibited the Catholic Church from hiring new castrati.

These young men shared their gifts with the world, only for the world to respond by killing their legacies. Get this—the world hasn't changed! This reminds me of Esau's story. Genesis 25:29-34 reads, "And Jacob sod pottage: and Esau came from the field, and he was faint: And Esau said to Jacob, Feed me, I pray thee, with that same red pottage; for I am faint: therefore was his name called Edom. And Jacob said, Sell me this day thy birthright. And Esau said, Behold, I am at the point to die: and what profit shall this birthright do to me? And Jacob said, Swear to me this day; and he sware unto him: and he sold his birthright unto Jacob. Then Jacob gave Esau bread and pottage of lentiles; and he did eat and drink, and rose up, and went his way: thus Esau despised his birthright." What was the significance of the birthright?

1. The first born son would receive a double portion of his father's inheritance.
2. The birthright brought with it certain privileges, rights and responsibilities; he would be considered the priest of the family upon his father's death.
3. The first born son carried on the judicial authority of his father.
4. The first-born was symbolic of Jesus Christ, who was and is the first begotten Son of God.

Esau was around 15-years old when he sold his birthright to his brother. He didn't understand the value of being an heir. This means that Esau was immature, and not because he was 15-years old. Esau's immaturity manifested in his decision to sell his birthright. By doing this, Esau essentially made himself a eunuch. And as despicable as his act may have been, it's actually a very common practice. You see, prophets and prophetic models (creatives) go through ages and stages. Just like stars, many of them are ready to begin burning their fuel the moment they realize that they are anointed, called, chosen—or whatever the case may be. When ambition is coupled with immaturity (lack of knowledge and experience), it often produces pride and anxiety (the fruit of anxiousness or impatience). Pride is a hard-outer shell that forms around the heart. All the same, anxiousness sets the stage for jealousy, competition, frustration and a host of other issues; this is what we call a stronghold. This is why the scriptures tell us that hope deferred makes the heart sick. When this happens, the proud individual's perception of the world, the church and his or her leader is severely altered. Gifts who are in the prepubescent stages of their gifting often believe:

1. Their leaders are resisting God by not giving them the stages and the opportunities they believe that they are ready for.
2. Their leaders are the reason that they are not as successful as they should be. This is because they see ministry as a career, rather than a responsibility to cover, love, teach and lead God's people.
3. Their leaders are intimidated by their potential, and as such, are intentionally hiding them from the world. They are known to refer to their leaders as "Sauls."
4. Their seasons are up at their local assemblies.
5. They don't need a pastor.

6. They are uniquely anointed, and this is why it is hard for other leaders to understand them.
7. They are smarter than their pastors.

But the truth of the matter is, a pastor, leader or any good mentor will always check the student's pitch to determine if he or she is ready to be revealed. Remember, when a star begins to form, it is often shielded by a molecular cloud (also called dark nebula). Within a molecular cloud, there are mounds of dust and gas cores called "clumps." These clumps slowly form into what we call protostars; that is, if there is enough gravitational energy within the cloud to cause the dust and the gas to collapse. (Note: most stars never truly emerge from these clouds because there isn't enough gravitational energy within the cloud. This means that the star doesn't have enough love or information to draw people to him or her). Stars form when the denser parts of the molecular cloud begin to collapse under its own weight and gravity. Now, remember, this is all happening within the cloud; no one can see the star and no one can hear the star just yet! If this process is not complete, the would-be star has no choice but to burn out before its time! Your pastor is your molecular cloud, of course. Your pastor's job is to check the pitch of your voice to determine whether or not you are ready for the next level. It doesn't matter if you're called to be great, you have to be humble enough to survive:

- the seasons of feeling overlooked and forgotten
- the seasons of seclusion
- the seasons of frustration
- the season of the test (temptation)

Let's look at another example. Luke 15:11-16 reads, "And he said, A certain man had two sons: And the younger of them said to his father, Father, give me the portion of goods that falleth to me. And he divided unto them his living. And not many days after the younger son gathered all together, and took his journey into a far country, and there wasted his substance with riotous living. And when he had spent all, there arose a mighty famine in that land; and he began to be in want. And he went and joined himself to a citizen of that country; and he sent him into his fields to feed swine. And he would fain have filled his belly with the husks that the swine did eat: and no man gave unto him." The Prodigal Son was a remarkable example of an immature star. Being the second born son of his father, he knew that his brother would receive the birthright, but as a son, he would still get an inheritance as well. Like most gifts in their youth, he began to imagine what life would be like if he had enough money to travel the world and do whatsoever he pleased without having to answer to anyone. His imaginations dominated his reality, and before long, he found himself standing in front of his father completely dishonoring him. Asking a living man for your inheritance was a slap in that man's face. Howbeit, the Prodigal Son did just that. His father, although grieved, complied with his wishes. Hear me—

when a father, a leader or a mentor gives you something that you are not mature enough to handle, they are doing it so that you can stop demonizing them and learn your lesson on your own! Because this is what some people need! No amount of talking, rebuking, hugging or begging will convince them to let God finish developing them. There are two types of students—one learns through studying and mentorship, the other learns through experience! The Prodigal Son needed to experience everything outside the cloud (his father) before he would be able to appreciate the cloud! And how did he respond? Days later, he left his father's house; he left his father's church! Get this—even if you give some people what they were asking for, they are going to leave! His heart towards his father had been altered by his perversion! He took his inheritance and spent it on riotous living. This means that there was a season when the prodigal son had absolutely no regrets! He was living the high life, partying and hanging out with his new crew until all of his money and energy had been spent! Where was his crew after that? Why didn't anyone invite him to live with them? Instead, he found himself having to go from being a son to a slave! Let's look at the four levels of a gift.

Slave	Servant	Steward	Son
Slaves do not own themselves, but are, instead, the "property" of another human being. Of course, in this context, a slave can also be the "property" of a taskmaster (their own flesh or a demonic spirit that manipulates and dominates the slave's movements and decisions). Slaves work freely; at best, they work in exchange for their lives or to have some sense of normalcy. A slave is considered to be the property of	Another word for "servant" is "employee." Servants consent to working for their employers in exchange for some form of currency, whether it's money, land or a place to stay. Jacob became Laban's servant in exchange for his daughter, Rachel's hand in marriage. Servants are not considered the property of their employers, meaning, they can quit their jobs or get promoted on their jobs.	A steward is a high-caliber servant. Think of it this way. In an organization such as a business or a church, there are levels of responsibilities. The difference between each level is called trust! A steward is given a small measure of responsibility, and if he stewards it well, his responsibilities and rank are increased within that organization. Of course, there are good stewards and	Another word for "son" is "heir." This is where we get the words heritage and hereditary. A son cannot be fired from his position, a son cannot stop his father from loving him, and a son is set to carry on the legacy of his father! Of course, when we use the terms son, him or his, this is also referring to women. Sons are not considered property or employees; they are representatives of their fathers. Sons are good stewards; they serve

| whomever or whatever is controlling him or her. | However, servants serve to get something in return. | not-so-good stewards. Poor stewards prove themselves to be servants. | because they love their fathers, not because of what they can get from him! |

Every leader has to check the fruit of the people serving him. Are you still a slave to your emotions and your lusts? Are you serving in your local assembly, and if so, why? Are you serving to get the attention of your pastor, to get promoted within the organization or are you serving because you love your leaders and want to help them to build their vision? Your motives reflect where you are on the spectrum! If you're serving for time or attention, you're still a servant! This isn't necessarily a bad thing; it simply means that you have some maturing to do! As time progresses, you will mature and your perspective will shift. Eventually, if you stay put and don't give up, you'll become a steward, graduate to a good steward and begin to operate as a son! A good steward or a son serves without complaining and without any hope of gain! When a leader or a father inspects your fruit, the leader isn't looking to see if you're mature physically, he or she is looking for spiritual fruits and the state those fruits are in! If you're still rolling your eyes at some of the folks you serve with, you aren't ready for a mic or a platform; you aren't ready to prophesy or lay hands on anyone because you need to be prophesying to yourself and laying hands on yourself in that season! Do you see the difference?! Leaders inspect fruit to ensure that you don't become developmentally delayed or spiritually delayed because when you share your gift with the world or the church at large, you will have to deal with high-level jealousy, high-level competition and high-ranking spirits! And if you're at the base of your calling, and you can't handle the pressure from there, it's only because you still have some growing to do! If you are revealed too quickly, the world will turn you into a spiritual castrato, meaning, you'll be gifted, but sterile! You'll become a slave of your own gifting! Hear me—any person who is a slave to his or her own gifting is a prostitute!

Castratos lost their abilities to reproduce; they lost their abilities to become fathers because the world got to sample their gifts prematurely. What frustrates leaders more than anything is watching prepubescent gifts rush out towards the spotlight, only to get burned out before their time. We have to see this time and time again, and it's excruciating to watch! What's even worse is when we feel helpless, watching a gift throw themselves at fame, riches and glory, not realizing that they are not emotionally, mentally or spiritually ready for the doors that they are trying to snatch open! This is why a leader has to check your pitch! And get this, your pitch isn't the range of your voice; it has nothing to do with how many people your voice can reach. It has everything to do with whether or not your voice has reached you! The first person you have to terraform is yourself, and if you can't accomplish this task, you are not yet ready for leadership!

If a young leader rushes out before his or her time, the world will stop the development of that gift; the world will castrate that gift! Look at some of your favorite celebrities from the eighties, nineties and the beginning of this millennium. Many of them are *still* wearing the costumes and sporting the mindsets that they wrapped themselves in during the highest points of their careers! They simply stopped growing, and now they've been typecast, meaning, they can never introduce the world to a new and developed version of themselves. In order to be accepted, they have to remain stuck in the realms that their fans celebrated them in! They have become the theatrical versions of castratos!

So, the question is, "When should I share my gift with the world?" The simple answer is—after you become the gift! The not-so-favorable answer is—after you have been cleared for take-off by the people who've been entrusted with overseeing your development! You have to graduate from a slave to a son, and you can't skip any steps along the way. Of course, I'm not talking about launching a business, I'm talking about taking on a leadership role in ministry or any organization that you want to advance in! If you want to launch a business, do it just as long as it does not violate your core values or the core values of the church. David said, "I encouraged myself in the Lord!" This is the mark of maturity; this is the mark of a leader!

The next question is, "What should I do if my pastor is not creating space for me to share my gift?" And again, by gift, we're dealing in the ministerial spectrum, not the entrepreneurial spectrum. If you feel that you are a prophet or maybe that you are prophetic, set up a meeting with your leader. Share your beliefs with the leader and allow him or her to guide you. Hear me—there is a 50/50 chance that you're not going to come out of that meeting satisfied! But you (not your pastor) have the sole responsibility of wrestling down your logic, emotions and perversions! Now, if you go to a church where there is no prophetic ministry or if you go to a church that does not believe in the existence of prophets today, look up some prophetic activations in your area. Be sure to be accountable with your leader, regardless of his or her beliefs! Remember, there is no sound in space! In other words, a star is developed in silence! As it collapses in on itself, no one is around to hear it screaming, but when it is revealed, it shines ever-so-brightly before the world! In other words, there will be times when it feels like the world and everyone in it cannot see your pain or hear your cries for help! You have to overcome all of the pits and snares that Satan sets before you. You do this through fasting, praying and just by being accountable!

Prophetic Sound Barriers

Sound moves at an amazing 343 meters per second; that's 770 miles per hour in normal climates! Any flying object that reaches or exceeds the speed of sound breaks what we call the sound barrier. What is the sound barrier? According to Merriam Webster, it is "a sudden large increase in aerodynamic drag that occurs as the speed of an aircraft approaches the speed of sound." Drag is a force that resists the movements of objects when they are in the air. The speed of light, on the other hand, is 186,282 miles per second; that's 670,616,629 miles per hour! Nothing can supersede the speed of light, not even sound. John 8:12 reads, "Then spake Jesus again unto them, saying, I am the light of the world: he that followeth me shall not walk in darkness, but shall have the light of life." Jesus is the light of the world. Think about that for a moment. He is the Word of God; He is the Revelation of God! Get this—He is the glory of God! If you were traveling at the speed of light, you could travel around the world seven times in one second! This is why our Lord is omnipresent (present in all places at all times, omnipotent (possessing all power) and omniscient (He knows everything). Howbeit, the speed of sound is 770 miles per hour; this means that it would take sound four hours to travel around the Earth. While this is fast, it does not come close to the speed of light. What we can take from this is, it doesn't take God even a minute to show up wherever we are at any given time; this is why He says, "I will never leave nor forsake you," but the Word of God travels at the speed of your obedience.

When an aircraft goes beyond 770 miles per hour, it breaks the sound barrier and releases a unique sound. This sound is called a sonic boom. A sonic boom is a thunder-like sound created anytime an object travels through the air faster than the speed of sound. As an aircraft travels through the air, it pushes the molecules in its path aside, creating a shockwave. This wave is similar to the waves that boats create in water while on the move. Of course, we can't see the waves that form in the air.

Ecclesiastes 3:1-8 is one of the most poetic scriptures in the Bible; it reads, "To every thing there is a season, and a time to every purpose under the heaven: A time to be born, and a time to die; a time to plant, and a time to pluck up that which is planted; a time to kill, and a time to heal; a time to break down, and a time to build up; a time to weep, and a time to laugh; a time to mourn, and a time to dance; a time to cast away stones, and a time to gather stones together; a time to embrace, and a time to refrain from embracing; a time to get, and a time to lose; a time to keep, and a time to cast away; a time to rend, and a time to sew; a time to keep silence, and a time to speak; a time to love, and a time to hate; a time of war, and a time of peace." What this means is, there is a season for every prophetic voice and prophetic model to be heard, seen or experienced. There is a season for every prophetic mantle to be released. There is a season for the heir to receive his or her inheritance, just as there is a season for the heir to not focus on an inheritance, but to instead, focus on learning. This is why Galatians 4:1-3 is one of my favorite scriptural texts; it states, "Now I say, That the heir, as long as he is a child, differeth nothing from a servant, though he be lord of all; but is under tutors and governors until the time appointed of the father. Even so we, when we were children, were in bondage under the elements of the world." When the text says that as long as the heir is a child, it's not dealing with his age in chronos time; it's talking about maturity. What this means is:

1. You are an heir. You aren't just an heir of God, but you stand to inherit a mantle or a grace from whomsoever you are serving under. But as long as you are immature, you are no different than a servant. Yes, even if you have been ordained! There are some licensed and ordained babies out there, and they whine every time they don't get their way! What the scripture is saying is this—as long as you are immature, there are some gifts you won't be able to open, some places you won't be able to go, some things you won't be able to do and some people you won't be able to walk with! The Word of the Lord for us all is to mature! Romans 8:19 says it like this, "For the earnest expectation of the creature waiteth for the manifestation of the sons of God."
2. An heir is ALWAYS under tutors and governors UNTIL the time appointed of the Father! This means that you can't raise yourself, man of God! You can't ordain yourself, woman of God! When the season comes for you to be revealed, the clouds that have been concealing you will empower you before revealing you! These clouds are your tutors and governors! But whenever you exceed the speed of sound or, better yet, God's timing for your life, there is a sound that is released; in the music world, they say, "You're singing in the wrong key!"

When a prophet or prophetic model is released in the right timing, the right sound is released, and a ripple effect takes place in the realm of the spirit. This sound parts seas, rains fire down from Heaven, opens blind eyes, raises the dead, casts out devils, heals the sick and brings revival to every sphere of the Earth! Hear me—the temptation to ordain yourself, the temptation to reveal yourself and the temptation to promote yourself is just that—temptation! How does God tell us to deal with temptation? He said to resist it! This implies that temptation is just another force that we deal with; it is a wind that pushes us in one direction, but to resist it, we can't go with the wind, we have to go against it! And get this—the highest ever recorded wind blew through New Hampshire in 1934, and it was 234 miles per hour! Sound travels at 770 miles per hour; this means that the Word of God is a force that the wind cannot resist! This is why devils bow down at the sound of His name; this is why the rocks will cry out if we are quiet at the sound of His name! Please take this to heart—you can't fail if you let the Spirit of God lead you! But to go with Him means to go against every other force of nature that tries to push you into mediocrity or any form of normalcy. When the timing is right, your pitch will be right. This means that you'll speak in love, you'll forgive without incentive and you'll pray without ceasing! When the timing is right, you'll break the enemy's sound barrier! This is why the scriptures say, "A word spoken in due season, how good is it!" Here's another amazing fact —the fastest human sense that we possess isn't seeing, it's hearing! This is because your senses are activated the moment light reaches your eyes or sound reaches your ears; they both have to be transmitted to your brain. Once a sound wave reaches your brain, it is able to recognize it in 0.05 seconds! It takes your brain 0.2 seconds to recognize light when it reaches your eyes! In other words, the people don't need to see you, they need to experience what you have in your mouth! They don't need you to show up in your alligator boots or your best wig; they just need you to show up! Remember, all of Earth and creation is waiting on you to realize who you are; we are waiting for your pitch to get just right! We are waiting for the prophets and the prophetic models who are not swallowed up by ambition, chased into seclusion by Jezebel, blinded by Delilah or castrated by this world; we are waiting for these men and women of God to rise up! This is how the Word of God will reach all four corners of the Earth! We keep saying that we want revival, not realizing that the word "revive" means to regain consciousness! We have to wake up before we can wake anyone else up! We have to grow up before we can grow anyone else up!

As a reminder, there is no sound in space. And in order for a space shuttle to stay in orbit, it has to travel at an alarming 17,500 to 18,000 miles per hour … consistently! The last word for you is "frequency." You have a pitch, you have a season and you have a gift, but for all of those things to work, you have to have a frequency. This represents your consistency! You have to be consistent in your message, consistent in your love and consistent in just showing up! This is why unreliable prophets and creatives rarely reach enough speed to ascend any of the Mountains of Influence. This is also why emotional prophets and creatives rarely defy the world's gravitational pull; they are always sucked into some drama, tossed to and fro by every wind of doctrine or in their prophetic spaceships attempting to get over someone else they shouldn't have been involved with. They are gifted, they are called and they are Christians, but they have become slaves of their gifts! They prefer spotlights over revelation, mics over mastery and blame over accountability. They are gifted, but they are in the trenches of entitlement, the ditches of desperation and the sewers of their pride. And while in these deep, dark places, they are entertaining themselves and others with their gifts; this is because the gifts and callings are without repentance! Are they saved? Of course! But they are also ineffective; they are powerless! They have more potential than they have power! They are in the depths of space where everyone is listening to them, but no one can truly hear them. They perform, they cast out devils and they pray, but this doesn't change the fact that they are in a ditch, a valley or a low place! I can't stress this enough—in order for you to become consistent, you will have to mature, and in order for you to mature, you have to study ... consistently! Be warned that the greatest and most effective trap that Satan has ever created is called normalcy! The second trap is called ambition! The third one is called lack of accountability (blame)! All of these traps are pits; they are valleys or graveyards that house the living. In all of these pits, you'll find prophets and prophetic models prophesying to one another, dancers captivating their audiences with their creative expressions, singers holding some of the longest notes and entrepreneurs making a killing on Wall Street. But get this—these are buried talents; they are drunk, religious, deaf and blind! How were they buried alive? It's simple. God created us from dust! Our flesh is nothing more than a pile of carefully knit together dust particles. So, when the scriptures deal with mountains, it's really dealing with our flesh! When Abraham ascended Mount Moriah, he essentially overcame his flesh! When Moses ascended Mount Sinai, he essentially overcame his flesh! When Noah's ark landed on Mount Ararat, this represented the glory of God resting on flesh! There are gifts out thee who are buried alive because they were so determined to show off their talents that they didn't realize that they are the talents! But they are buried underneath their desires, their fears, their pasts and their rejection! This is why they need you to grow up and show up! They need someone who can look past their rough exteriors and exclaim, "There's something down there!" They need someone who's willing to reach past their potential to pull out their power! They need someone who can see past their insecurities, their carefully crafted facial expressions and their current conditions. This is why prophets and apostles have to get their hands dirty! We have to reach into filth and dig out the riches underneath the grime! Consistency builds trust, not only with your leaders, but with those who take a risk at following you. No consistency, no trust. Elisha couldn't just show up whenever he wanted to show up. He had to follow Elijah everywhere he went! And he had to do this without complaining! We have the internet now, so you can follow your Elijah's social media posts and make sure you're physically present at every local event that he or she teaches at. When you become a consistent follower, you'll become a consistent leader. And just so you know, another word for "consistent" is "faithful." The word "faithful" is just another extension of "faith." It simply means that you have so much faith that you're willing to inconvenience yourself to do the will of God. This is supernatural within itself! Every time you get out of bed on a Tuesday or a Wednesday night to go to Bible study, you are engaging the supernatural; you are defying your own natural desires so that you can position yourself in an atmosphere of worship. This is what makes it supernatural! The word "super" in this text means "above" or "beyond." Anytime you go beyond your flesh's desires and anytime you forsake your own convenience to spend time in God's presence or with His people, you are literally engaging the supernatural.

Take your time. Let God develop you. Move at the speed of sound (God's voice in your life). When your season to be revealed comes, God will lift you up in the same manner He lifted Noah's ark, and He will bring you out of your cloud. This is when you'll shine like the star you are, and you won't be willing to sell your birthright for a bowl of normalcy! When your pitch is just right, when your frequency is just right and when the season is just right, you'll become a rare gift, and get this—rare gifts move faster than the speed of light whenever they are doing the will of God! How so? Because they move with God and He is the light of the world!

Prophetic Activation

Slave	Servant	Steward	Son

This activation can be tricky because it involves you putting away your pride, and just being honest with yourself. Based on what you learned in this chapter, would you say that you are a slave, servant, steward or son! If you're unsure, ask your pastor, your mentor or someone on the leadership team at your church! And do NOT be offended with their answer!

Mission Nine

T-01

Dark Matter and Black Holes

Have you ever heard the phrase, "Hurt people hurt people?" Of course, you have! And through experience, we all know this to be true! The heart is the mirror of the soul. Anything that happens to the heart reflects in through our language, our choices, our relationships and our lives as a whole; that is, of course, if we are not healed. Our hearts are not like Vegas. Whatever happens in the heart doesn't stay there; instead, it projects itself like a force field around us and essentially becomes our worlds. It becomes the lens by which we see life. So, if someone hurts you, you essentially become a "hurt person." You graduate from being hurt to being hurtful.

Ascension	Hurt	Hurt-filled	Hurtful

We've discussed a lot of laws in this book, but there are some scriptural laws as well. As a matter of fact, everything science says (that is true, of course), God already said! Scientists simply use a different set of words to explain what we already know or should know. Anything God says is a statute; it's more than a fact, it's a law! It's established in Heaven and it travels at the speed of light. It cannot and will not return to Him void. The word "void" means empty, dark or absent of light. In other words, it cannot return to Him until it has accomplished His will and performed His Word in every life that it has touched. So again, if you're hurt and you don't deal with that hurt expeditiously, you'll be promoted from being hurt to becoming hurtful. So, why do hurt people hurt people? In physics, they call it gravity. Gravity is defined as "the force that attracts a body toward the center of the earth, or toward any other physical body having mass" (Source: Google). But it's more complicated than that. This is where Newton's Law of Universal Gravitation comes to play. It states that "every particle attracts every other particle in the universe with a force which is directly proportional to the product of their masses and inversely proportional to the square of the distance between their centers" (Source: Wikipedia/Newton's Law of Universal Gravitation). What I'm doing is using "their" language to describe a Kingdom principle! Before you got saved, you may have heard it this way, "Birds of a feather flock together!" In the Kingdom language, we say "As a man thinks in his heart, so is he." But let's dive a little deeper into this. These are all the same phrases in three different languages!

Your soul is comprised of your mind, will and emotions. Your mind has three levels; they are the conscious, subconscious and unconscious. Whenever you experience trauma, that trauma impacts your mind or, better yet, the way that you think, reason and perceive the world. Low-level trauma puts a dent in your subconscious; consequently, it alters one or more of your belief systems. For example, if you keep losing friends, you may begin to reason that most, if not all, humans are incapable of being "true friends." As a result of this belief, you may try to live your life in solitude, always referring to people as your "associates" or "peers." This would make it nearly impossible for you to be friendly, and therefore, it'll be nearly impossible for you to have friends. Not receiving any friends then confirms your belief that humans are incapable of being friends, thus, causing you to believe that you're the only human left with a set of morals intact. This isn't true and, of course, it leads to pride. This is why the scriptures tell us to not think any higher of ourselves than we should! If the trauma is severe enough, it reaches in and impacts your conscious mind. This is when people start reacting without thinking. For example, if you've experienced a traumatic event with a former friend, you may explode whenever one of your current friends says or does something that triggers that memory. Because of this, you'll only attract what you believe and agree with! So, hurt people don't just hurt people, they gravitate towards other hurt people, and the one who's pain, anger or bitterness is more defined is likely the one who will do the most damage. What's this called? It's called reproduction! Hurt people reproduce their pain! Every issue in a man's heart is designed to reproduce itself! You'll notice that, in the wild, eagles aren't romantically attracted to ducks, even though they're both birds! Why is this? Because they have no agreement. One likes high places, the other likes low places. One likes ditches, the other likes mountaintops. So, the theory that opposites attract isn't absolute. Opposites don't always attract; in some cases, they actually repel one another. So, when you see two people romantically linked together who appear to be as opposite as night and day, please understand that they have a pull (agreement) somewhere that may not be readily available to the naked eye. They may be attracted to each other's differences as well, but there is something in the both of them that draws them together, even if it's rebellion! As a pastor, I'm not deceived into believing that a member with a good heart and good intentions is dating a broken man. Sure, she may be nice, she may be faithful and she may even be a decent person, but her choice of a man tells me where she's at on the maturity spectrum. There's something in her that attracted him, and there's something in him that attracted her. So, if he does what hurt people do—if he breaks her heart, I don't waste my time trying to usher her into healing by flattering her pain. She needs the truth; the scriptures say that it is the truth that sets us free. In other words, I point her to a book! So, the short answer is gravity. If she changes her diet (what she reads, who she surrounds herself with, what she's entertained by), she'll simultaneously change what she's attracted to and vice versa.

Get this—the soul splits. Most pastors who engage the ministry of deliverance are aware of this. Most psychiatrists, psychologists, psychotherapists and most of the people who study the mind are aware of this. But as a church, we've lived in the dark for a long time. This is why God says, "My people perish for lack of knowledge." If a person goes through a traumatic enough event, it does and will affect that person's mind, will and emotions. We see this, but we don't like to talk too much about it because, as the church, we're afraid of any information that has the word "science" attached to it, not realizing that science is nothing but low-level truths broken down into a consistency that allows us to digest them. They are called facts. There are scientists who are pagan; they hate the Word and they are always trying to disprove it, but true scientists almost always end up Christian because the low-level truths (facts) always leads them to God. Of course, there are some Christian scientists who become agnostic or atheist, but the scriptures tell us why this happens! God gave them over to reprobate minds because they changed the truth of God into a lie, and they loved the creature more than the Creator (see Romans 1:25). What this literally means is, there are scientists out there who were surrounded by their pagan colleagues, but they were Christians. They wanted so badly to ascend the ranks in their organizations and establish their names in high places that they didn't publish the results that they found if those results pointed the people towards God! Instead, they worked diligently to prove God wrong! Hear me—there are scientists out there who've admitted to doing this!

But again, trauma does impact their souls. And of course, we were all born with one soul, but if it endures enough trauma, it can and does split. This causes what doctors refer to as multiple-personality disorder, schizophrenia, dissociative personality disorder and so on. As a matter of fact, the prefix "schizo" means "split" or "division" and the suffix "phrenia" means "the mind." So, schizophrenia means to split, separate or divide the mind. James 1:8 says, "A double minded man is unstable in all his ways." The Hebrew word used for "mind" is the Greek word "psuche," which is where we get the word "psyche." This word corresponds with the Hebrew word "nephesh" and it literally means soul. So, the scripture can be read this way, "A man with two souls is unstable in every way." But the question is, if God gave us one soul, how does a person end up double-minded or with two souls? The answer is—trauma! Think about the impact of two cars hitting one another. Most cars don't split in an accident, but they can be severely damaged. And of course, there have been many cars that were so impacted by another vehicle, especially a vehicle greater in size being driven at a high rate of speed, that have been split in two or more pieces! This brings us to another one of Isaac Newton's laws! This one is called the Law of Restitution; this law states that when two objects collide, their speeds after the collision are determined by the materials from which they were made. What were you made of before you got hurt? Were you filled with rage, anger, lust and gossip? If so, the trauma created a wound in your soul called a void. The rage, anger, lust and issues that you had started to fill that void, thus, attracting other rage-filled, angry and perverted folks into your life. Or were you filled with love, joy, understanding and wisdom? If so, the trauma created a wound in your soul, but the love in you filled that wound; that is, if the force behind the impact didn't shift your thinking in the wrong direction. The gravity from the trauma is going to either pull you closer to God or it will drive you further away from Him. But the gravity does something else, after all, you are a star. And when a star begins to collapse within itself, its gravitational pull increases! Think about this—have you ever noticed that every time your heart was broken, you knew exactly who to call? Especially if you didn't understand the trauma and you wanted to get even with the person or people who hurt you! You didn't call that friend who would love on you and tell you a truth you didn't want to hear. You called that broken friend who would load up her weapon and catch a flight at the mere sound of pain. Did she do this because she was a great friend? Absolutely not! She did it because she could relate to you! She did this because of a biblical law, described in Amos 3:3, which states, "Can two walk together, except they be agreed?" The hurt in you was so astronomical that it began to behave like gravity; being near you was almost irresistible to her. She wanted to hear everything you'd gone through because, get this, she was hurting too! But your pain helped her to forget her own issues! Of course, there are some good friends out there who will catch a flight just to support you. The easiest way to differentiate the two is by calling your friend and telling her all of your great news as well. If she reacts negatively or rushes you off the phone, it's because nothing in what you said had any type of magnetic pull on her! In other words, she couldn't relate to you! You guessed it! This deals with another law of physics called the Law of Reflection!

Dictionary.com defines the Law of Reflection this way, "The principle that when a ray of light, radar pulse, or the like, is reflected from a smooth surface the angle of reflection is equal to the angle of incidence, and the incident ray, the reflected ray, and the normal to the surface at the point of incidence all lie in the same plane." In other words, you attract what you are! This is why when you're ascending one of the Mountains of Influence, you'll find yourself losing friends! This isn't for everyone; I'm speaking to climbers! Every time your mind changes, the people who agreed with your former mindset have to find new ground in your life. If the two of you can't find something else equal to or greater than the size of your former agreement, you will grow apart! This leaves a void or an empty place in both of your lives. This void has a strong gravitational pull; it not only attracts people who are on the level you're on now, but it also attracts people from your former season. This is because your soul is still, at that point, filled with the residue of yesterday, and that residue is magnetic!

Marriages can be divided by trauma as well. When two people marry, they don't instantaneously become one person, they grow together. As they are growing together, they form a unified body called a marriage. The marriage is everything they agree about, but the division in the marriage is everything that they don't agree about. Their goal is to unify wherever they could, and to respect the other areas where they don't necessarily agree. If they agree to respect one another, that agreement could supersede their disagreements! There are

two ways to resolve disagreements in marriage, and they are:
1. to agree to disagree.
2. to both seek the truth with an open heart. You will always unify in the truth!

But during those events that we call "disagreements," it is common for one of the spouses to say or do something that, not only traumatizes the other spouse, but puts a dent in the marriage. Like the soul, when a marriage has been impacted, a gravity-like force is emitted. This attracts the wrong people and the right people. But if you're hurt, you'll likely gravitate towards the wrong people if the size of your hurt is greater than or equal to the measure of love that you have. And finally, governments can split; this is why we have civil wars. Anything that can be seen or felt can be split! And anytime a split occurs, a black hole is created! When a marriage is divided, a black hole is created! When a soul is divided, a black hole is created; this hole is called a void! When a government is divided, a black hole is created! And these black holes suck in any and everyone who comes within a certain range; this range is called agreement! This is why Ahab asked Jehoshaphat, "Will you go with me to fight against Ramoth Gilead?" How did Jehoshaphat respond? He said, "I am as you are, my people as your people, my horses as your horses." Because Jehoshaphat was so determined to win favor with Ahab, he kept getting sucked into Ahab's plans! This is because Ahab was a black hole! Another example of a black hole was Absalom, the son of David! 2 Samuel 15:1-6 reads, "And it came to pass after this, that Absalom prepared him chariots and horses, and fifty men to run before him. And Absalom rose up early, and stood beside the way of the gate: and it was so, that when any man that had a controversy came to the king for judgment, then Absalom called unto him, and said, Of what city art thou? And he said, Thy servant is of one of the tribes of Israel. And Absalom said unto him, See, thy matters are good and right; but there is no man deputed of the king to hear thee. Absalom said moreover, Oh that I were made judge in the land, that every man which hath any suit or cause might come unto me, and I would do him justice! And it was so, that when any man came nigh to him to do him obeisance, he put forth his hand, and took him, and kissed him. And on this manner did Absalom to all Israel that came to the king for judgment: so Absalom stole the hearts of the men of Israel." Who did Absalom call to him? The men who had a controversy! People who were dissatisfied with how the kingdom had been run!

As a prophet or creative, you have to be cognizant of the fact that the enemy wants you outside of God's will so that God's glory won't radiate through you. He wants to rush you into relationships, into ministry and into an early grave! He wants to surround you with tares and rush you up the Mountains of Influence. Hear me—he wants you to become double-minded; he wants you to become a black hole! This way, you will be partly Christian, but the other half of you will love the profane things of this world! This makes you unstable, and when God sees this, He knows that He can't trust you with power and influence! So, God has to hold you back, even though you're exerting all of your energy and effort to go forth! Do you see how stars burn out? Do you understand how voids are created? But a void is like an empty stomach; it causes you to hunger for what you cannot have all the more! It causes you to long for everything you're not mature enough to possess! It makes you want power, influence and anything that has the ability to crush you! So, the more God holds you back, the hungrier you get! He's trying to protect you, but the enemy wants to use your ambition, your hurt or your impatience to destroy you! This is why Proverbs 16:18 warns us, "Pride goes before destruction, a haughty spirit before a fall." What I'm trying to tell you is this—just like souls split, marriages split and governments split, please understand that churches can and do split! They split when black holes are created within the organization! They split when leaders who've exerted all of their energy wrestling with God begin to suck other members and leaders in with their lies and half-truths! These leaders spin the truth and create false narratives!

There are many reasons that churches divide or split, but the most common culprits are church members who have an insidious, almost insatiable need for power and fame. This is why I placed so much emphasis on the fruit of long-suffering (patience) in this book! Most church splits are the result of a leader who's said in his or her heart, "I will ascend above the rank of the pastor! I will be like the senior leader!" That leader then goes about sweeping the floors, ironing the pastor's clothes and doing whatsoever he or she has to do to win favor with the pastor. Hear me—it rarely works! Any good pastor with a prayer life and a little experience can smell ambition and can see envy in the earliest stages of development, after all, they both have a rhythm! A rhythm is a pattern. They both have an accent; the accent represents a unique sound! In other words, we've seen it before! We've experienced it before! There is nothing new underneath the sun, but it's hard to convince most people of this! So, while the pastor continues to thank the helpful leader for everything he's doing, he (for example) promotes his sons and daughters when the time is right. This ignites the ambitious leader's fury, and once that candle has been lit, it is difficult to put it out. Proverbs 18:19 confirms this; it reads, "A brother offended is harder to win than a strong city, and contentions are like the bars of a castle." Offense has five stages. They are:
- **Stage 1:** Confusion
- **Stage 2:** Comparison
- **Stage 3:** Frustration
- **Stage 4:** Aggravation
- **Stage 5:** Wrath

Stage #	Stage Name	Characteristics
Stage 1	Confusion	This is the "why" stage. Normally, during this phase, the person asks a lot of questions, not just to himself or herself, but to others. These questions often lead to gossip, slander and more confusion.
Stage 2	Comparison	During these discussions, the spirit of competition enters the equation. The offended party starts saying things like, "If it were me" or "If I was the pastor." They even begin to compare themselves to the leaders filling the roles that they want. Comparison always leads to competition, and when they start competing, they start doing things like usurping the senior leader's authority, performing tasks assigned to other leaders or being negligent in the roles that they have. For example, they start reasoning that if they are not present or if they don't do their jobs, the whole ministry will fall apart. In other words, the spirit of sabotage also enters the equation.
Stage 3	Frustration	When their futile attempts to get answers to their many questions or to sabotage the ministry are unsuccessful, the offended party begins to collapse within himself or herself. This is the stage of frustration, and it is also further aggravated when the party observes the very issues he or she has been complaining about still flourishing. These can be actual issues that should be addressed, or they could be a product of the offended party's imagination. During this stage, they start plotting more, talking more and doing less!
Stage 4	Aggravation	Frustration is the state of being annoyed, but aggravation is the state of being or feeling provoked. The prophet or prophetic model, at this stage, has been making their grievances known either directly or indirectly. During this phase, the offended party has either taken to looking at other churches, speaking with other leaders, visiting other churches and posting passive-aggressive statuses on social media in an attempt to either get their leaders' attention or to sow a seed in the hearts of the other members. During this phase, it is difficult, if not impossible, for the offended party to hide his or her frustration, ambition and everything else that's been growing in his or her

Stage #	Stage Name	Characteristics
		heart. This is because these issues all represent trees, and the season has come where these trees are beginning to bear fruit.
Stage 5	Wrath	The offended party has now left the church or is still in the church, intentionally trying to turn the hearts of the other leaders and members towards himself or herself. In some cases, if they don't have a plan to build another church, they will begin to point members to one of the churches they've been visiting. They'll say things like, "I went to a church down in Macon, and I've never heard such great preaching before! Girl, the man of God prophesied over me, and when he prayed for me, I fell all the way out! God is truly in that place! There were so many miracles taking place that I didn't know what to do! Come with me next Sunday!" The goal here is to divide the church; the goal here is to sabotage everything that the senior leader is building.

Isaiah 14:12-20: How art thou fallen from heaven, O Lucifer, son of the morning! How art thou cut down to the ground, which didst weaken the nations! For thou hast said in thine heart, I will ascend into heaven, I will exalt my throne above the stars of God: I will sit also upon the mount of the congregation, in the sides of the north: I will ascend above the heights of the clouds; I will be like the most High. Yet thou shalt be brought down to hell, to the sides of the pit. They that see thee shall narrowly look upon thee, and consider thee, saying, Is this the man that made the earth to tremble, that did shake kingdoms; that made the world as a wilderness, and destroyed the cities thereof; that opened not the house of his prisoners? All the kings of the nations, even all of them, lie in glory, everyone in his own house. But thou art cast out of thy grave like an abominable branch, and as the raiment of those that are slain, thrust through with a sword, that go down to the stones of the pit; as a carcass trodden under feet. Thou shalt not be joined with them in burial, because thou hast destroyed thy land, and slain thy people: the seed of evildoers shall never be renowned.

Revelation 12:3-4: And there appeared another wonder in heaven; and behold a great red dragon, having seven heads and ten horns, and seven crowns upon his heads. And his tail drew the third part of the stars of heaven, and did cast them to the earth: and the dragon stood before the woman which was ready to be delivered, for to devour her child as soon as it was born.

When the aforementioned scripture refers to a third part of the stars in Heaven, it was literally talking about angels. When Lucifer fell, a third of the angels fell with him. This is because he'd led a revolt in Heaven. But why did an angel who had everything he needed decide to give it all up? Ezekiel 28:13-19 gives us some insight; it reads, "Thou hast been in Eden the garden of God; every precious stone was thy covering, the sardius, topaz, and the diamond, the beryl, the onyx, and the jasper, the sapphire, the emerald, and the carbuncle, and gold: the workmanship of thy tabrets and of thy pipes was prepared in thee in the day that thou wast created. Thou art the anointed cherub that covereth; and I have set thee so: thou wast upon the holy mountain of God; thou hast walked up and down in the midst of the stones of fire. Thou wast perfect in thy ways from the day that thou wast created, till iniquity was found in thee. By the multitude of thy merchandise they have filled the midst of thee with violence, and thou hast sinned: therefore I will cast thee as profane out of the mountain of God: and I will destroy thee, O covering cherub, from the midst of the stones of fire. Thine heart was lifted up because of thy beauty, thou hast corrupted thy wisdom by reason of thy brightness: I will cast thee to the ground, I will lay thee before kings, that they may behold thee. Thou hast defiled thy sanctuaries by the multitude of thine iniquities, by the iniquity of thy traffick; therefore will I bring forth a fire from the midst of thee, it shall devour thee, and I will bring thee to ashes upon the earth in the sight of all them that behold thee. All they that know thee among the people shall be astonished at thee: thou shalt be a terror, and never shalt thou be any more."

Lucifer was covered with precious stones. He had been adorned with rubies, topaz, diamonds, emeralds and almost every precious stone you could think of. He was beautiful to behold! His body was God's instrument, filled with pipes, harps and timbrels. His job was to gather the angels together, and whenever the winds of God blew through him and the glory of God radiated through him, the angels would bow before him. Of course, they weren't reverencing him, they were worshiping God, but Lucifer convinced himself that they were worshiping him, after all, he didn't just have a gift, he was a gift. His body had been a beautifully crafted instrument of worship. Whenever the glory of God radiated from the jewels, the light would pierce the atmosphere and the angels would cry out in worship. He loved how powerful he felt in those moments; he loved seeing the angels bowing before him and he coveted God's position and power. This is how iniquity made its way into his heart. When iniquity entered his heart, it began to bend his pipes. He then began to reason within himself that he too could be powerful—he could be even greater than God! He sold his idea to a bunch of angels, promising them positions of power. He convinced them that they were being mistreated by God and a New Heaven Order would even the playing field. Many of the angels considered his words and immediately became dissatisfied with their positions. When God gathered the angels for worship, Lucifer's pipes had been bent by perversion, meaning, he didn't sound the same and many of the angels didn't respond the same. Instead, Lucifer released a sound of perversion, one that was vile and profane. This is why the scriptures say that perversion was found in him. After this, the scriptures tell us that there was a war in Heaven. Revelation 12:7-9 says, "And there was war in heaven: Michael and his angels fought against the dragon; and the dragon fought and his angels, and prevailed not; neither was their place found any more in heaven. And the great dragon was cast out, that old serpent, called the Devil, and Satan, which deceiveth the whole world: he was cast out into the earth, and his angels were cast out with him." In the same manner he'd deceived Eve, he'd managed to deceive a third of God's angels. In other words, Satan had become a black hole. What Satan attempted in Heaven is the equivalent of what we, in the world of ministry, call a church split.

What exactly is a black hole? "A black hole is a place in space where gravity pulls so much that even light cannot get out. The gravity is so strong because matter has been squeezed into a tiny space. This can happen when a star is dying" (Nasa.gov/ What is a Black Hole?/Heather R. Smith/NASA Educational Technology Services). Earlier on, we discussed the life cycle of a star. Let's look at how black holes are created to get a better understanding of how Lucifer became Satan, and how churches are split and relationships are destroyed.

Star One Cycle	Stellar Nebula	Main Sequence	Red Giant	Planetary Nebula	White Dwarf
Star Two Cycle	Stellar Nebula	Main Sequence	Red Super Giant	Supernova	Neutron / Black Hole

Star One Cycle

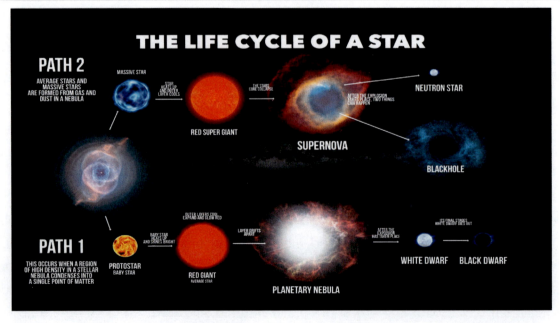

Stellar Nebula: This is the place where stars are born! Named after the Latin word for "cloud," stellar nebula are also called "stellar nurseries." Inside of these clouds are clusters of protostars in their varying processes of formation. Many of them will grow to become main sequence stars, while others will never have enough energy in their cores to follow suit. The ones who don't grow into main sequence stars become brown dwarfs.

Main Sequence: Around ninety percent of the stars in our universe are main sequence stars; this includes our sun. Main sequence stars are all undergoing the fusion of hydrogen into helium within their cores. The mass of a star determines the lifespan of that star. Gravity is the force inside the star, and it is balanced by the outward forces of gas pressure and radiation pressure. The more massive the star is, the greater its gravitational pull inwards.

Red Giant: This is a giant star in its last phase of stellar evolution. During this phase, the star expands, growing many times its original size. When the hydrogen supply in the core is exhausted, there is nothing left to counter the effects of gravity. When the hydrogen fuel in the star's core has been exhausted, nuclear reactions will take place, all of which will move outward. It will then begin to burn the hydrogen that's surrounding the core. Consequently, the outside of the star will start to expand; this causes it to cool down and take on a red glow. Red Giants normally grow to more than 400 times their original size!

Planetary Nebula: As the Red Giant burns up its fuel, it will eventually collapse in on itself. The outer layers will expand into space and form a ring of clouds called planetary nebula. Note: the word "planetary" is a misnomer; they looked like planetary disks when viewed through the instruments in the seventies. This is why they were named planetary nebula.

White Dwarf: Normally the size of a planet, these small and very dense stars are what stars become after they have burned through all of their nuclear fuel. After stars have burned through their outer material, nothing but the core remains. This core is called a White Dwarf.

Star Two Cycle

Stellar Nebula: (see above description)
Main Sequence: (see above description)
Red Super Giant: The largest and most massive stars in the universe, Red Super Giants form when a massive star (a star with more than ten solar masses) runs out of hydrogen fuel in its core. Consequently, the core begins to fill with helium, causing the star to collapse within itself. This increases the temperature of the star, which in turn, causes the outer layers of the star to expand and cool off. This is what causes the red glow.

Supernova: A Supernova, in layman's terms, is the explosion of a star. When the core of a Red Super Giant becomes so full of itself, it is unable to withstand its own gravitational force; this causes the core to collapse. The star then explodes and creates a Supernova.

Neutron: When a star isn't massive enough to form into a black hole, it becomes a Neutron star. A Neutron star is the residue of a giant star after its explosion. About the size of a city, the gravitational pull of a Neutron star is two billion times stronger than the gravity on Earth. These spinning stars can rotate as fast as 43,000 times per minute, but they lose their momentum over time.

Black Hole: These former stars are some of the most complex and mysterious formations in our galaxy! When a star burns up the remnants of its fuel, the core then collapses or falls into itself. This either forms into a Neutron star (if it isn't massive enough), but if it is massive, it creates a vacuum called a black hole. There are two types of black holes; they are Stellar Black Holes and Supermassive Black Holes.

- **Stellar Black Hole:** These black holes are created by the collapse of individual, relatively small stars. Even though they are incredibly dense, they have more than three times the mass of the sun, compacted into the size of a small city. This is why the gravitational pull around these black holes is so strong. Stellar Black Holes, like Massive Black Holes, consume the dust and gas from the galaxies that surround them; this causes the black hole to grow in size, thus allowing it to consume more dust and gas.
- **Supermassive Black Hole:** These black holes are believed to be the result of hundreds or maybe even thousands of Stellar Black Holes that have merged together. These black holes have masses that are millions and even billions of times more massive than our sun! Scientists aren't fully sure how these stars formed, but again, one theory is that they are the result of smaller black holes merging together. Another theory is that large gas clouds may have merged together because of their gravitational pulls, and these clouds may have also collapsed together. The final theory is that they are the result of the collapse of a stellar cluster; these are a group of stars that fell together.

Lucifer was already a big star in Heaven. Again, he was the worship leader in Heaven, and he was massive! He would gather the angels together to worship God; his body would radiate God's glory, and his instruments would sing some of the most beautiful sounds of worship ever to be heard. The angels would bow before him, but not to him. They worshiped the King of kings and the Lord of lords, but Lucifer wanted this worship for himself. So, like the massive star he was, pride begin to bend his instruments. He kept collapsing within himself until he became a supermassive black hole. God watched as a third of His angels turned their backs on Him to stand on Lucifer's side. Lucifer was convinced that God needed him. He was so impressed with himself, his gift and his abilities that he didn't think of the possible consequence of his rebellion. He believed that there was strength in numbers. If he could get the majority of God's angels on his side, he believed that he could split Heaven and start his own kingdom. His imaginations were perverted, and his heart grew more and more dark. When the scriptures say that there was no place more found in Heaven for him, it's literally dealing with his heart. His heart had grown so massively wicked that it stuck out like a castrato's rib cage. He had to be expelled from Heaven, along with the angels who supported his "ministry." He'd sucked these angels into a lie, and now, these black holes are all over the Earth, consuming believers and non-believers alike. In the church, the enemy forms a black hole, once again, through incredibly ambitious souls who—get this—are truly anointed and called to the forefront of ministry. But they are tired of serving, tired of waiting and tired of being second, third or seventh in line! Not realizing that their hearts are rapidly growing more and more wicked, they justify their evil deeds with:

1. I cast out demons too!
2. I've healed people too!
3. I can preach too!
4. I've served my pastor for (x) amount of time, and I've done so faithfully!
5. The pastor promoted someone else above me who's not nearly as anointed as I am!
6. The pastor promoted someone else above me who hasn't been in this church nearly as long as I have!
7. A friend of mine served his pastor for (x) amount of years, and he's already the executive pastor!

They find people to share their grievances with, and these people agree with them. This increases the mass of the black hole that's growing in their hearts! Hear me—no amount of sound reasoning can reach them at this point because—get this—black holes eat everything, including light, and light represents revelation! They suck up the truth like a vacuum, never considering the information being shared with them! Slowly, but surely, they begin to split the churches that they once promised to uphold. They also find people who don't necessarily agree with them, and when this happens, their assignments are to sow seeds of discord in their hearts. Seeds grow over time! Proverbs 6:16-19 says, "These six things doth the LORD hate: yea, seven are an abomination unto him: A proud look, a lying tongue, and hands that shed innocent blood, an heart that deviseth wicked imaginations, feet that be swift in running to mischief, a false witness that speaketh lies, and he that soweth discord among brethren." Why does God hate false witnesses who sow discord among brethren? Because they reproduce the very event that Lucifer produced in Heaven when he'd approached God's angels and the very event that Satan produced on Earth when he'd approached Eve in the Garden! Every issue has to reproduce itself in order for it to continue, including black holes! But here's the thing about black holes; they don't just eat up the stars around them, but they continue to grow! Scientists once believed that black holes were permanent fixtures in our galaxy, but a man by the name of Stephen Hawking pretty much dispelled this myth! First off, let's establish this fact—black holes have what's called an event horizon and a singularity. Let's look at their definitions.

- **Singularity:** "a one-dimensional point which contains a huge mass in an infinitely small space, where density and gravity become infinite and space-time curves infinitely, and

where the laws of physics as we know them cease to operate. As the eminent American physicist Kip Thorne describes it, 'it is the point where all laws of physics break down'" (Source: The Physics of the Universe/ Singularities).
- **Event horizon:** "boundary marking the limits of a black hole. At the event horizon, the escape velocity is equal to the speed of light. Since general relativity states that nothing can travel faster than the speed of light, nothing inside the event horizon can ever cross the boundary and escape beyond it, including light" (Source: Encyclopedia Britannica).

The singularity is the center of the black hole. Remember, we discussed earlier that mankind has no dominion in space. Our ability to travel within certain realms of outer space is the interstellar equivalent of grace. However, black holes have a singularity where the laws of physics as we know them do not apply. In other words, a black hole is a world (system) where our laws, principles and knowledge are all useless! Next, let's deal with the event horizon. Scientists previously believed (and still publish) that nothing can escape the event horizon, but again, a renown British scientist by the name of Stephen Hawking completely wrecked this theory! According to science, no information can escape past the event horizon, but Hawking Radiation is a theory published by Mr. Hawking. Scholarpedia tells us exactly what Hawking Radiation is; it states, "Hawking radiation is the thermal radiation predicted to be spontaneously emitted by black holes. It arises from the steady conversion of quantum vacuum fluctuations into pairs of particles, one of which escaping at infinity while the other is trapped inside the black hole horizon. It is named after the physicist Stephen Hawking who derived its existence in 1974. This radiation reduces the mass of black holes and is therefore also known as black hole evaporation" (Source: Scholarpedia/Hawking Radiation).

This theory totally shakes up black hole physics! In other words, Stephen Hawking theorized that not only can information escape the pits of a black hole, but it can also carry mass away from the black hole, causing it to slowly begin to evaporate! This information is called electromagnetic radiation, for example, light. It's referred to as "information" because it contains information about what has fallen into the event horizon. How does this translate into our discussion? It's simple! If you've fallen into the clutches of someone who has become a black hole, it may feel impossible, and it may be extremely difficult to escape their clutches, but hear me—you can get free! James 4:7 tells us how! "Submit yourselves therefore to God. Resist the devil, and he will flee from you." What God is telling us to apply Kingdom laws, since every other law is subject to the Kingdom! John 1:5 tells us, "And the light shineth in darkness; and the darkness comprehended it not." In other words, when you find yourself in a dark conversation, start talking about love, forgiveness and mercy! When folks start gossiping in your ear, don't let them suck you in! Start praising God and speaking life in their presence! In this, there are two different languages and laws being applied! But the Word of God has already prevailed! And please, hear my heart—every leader in every stage of his or her development feels all of the gravitational pulls around them as they ascend the Mountains of Influence! Every pastor can share endless stories about people from their worship departments leaving because another church was willing to give them more solos than their former churches had given them. These are gravitational pulls! The Kingdom word for gravity in this sense is called TEMPTATION! Some Christians resist it, but a large majority give into it. The ones who stand their ground, on the other hand, grow stronger, wiser and better! And while their former counterparts find themselves on a few more flyers and a few more stages, those who are faithful are graced with God's trust! Remember, the currency of the Kingdom of God is trust, and it can be used in every world and on every mountain! Trust provokes God to give you more; we witness this in the parable of the talents! Trust provokes God to take you into new worlds and cause you to flourish in them; we witness this in Joseph's story as well as Queen Esther's story! Trust provokes God to show you more; we witness this in Moses' life! When God sees that He can trust you with an opportunity, when He can trust you with favor and when He can trust you with material wealth, He starts piling it on you all the more! He piles more opportunities on you, He piles more favor on you and He piles more riches on you! This is God's trust; this is the currency of the Kingdom! You can't manipulate your way into it, cry your way into it or lie your way into it; you have to sow your way in, and more than that, when you ascend the mountains you're called to, you have to resist everything that's competing for your trust and attention! There will be times when everything in you wants to stop, everything in you wants to give up and everything in you wants to doubt God and die, but hear me, this is just gravity—it's just TEMPTATION! Resist it and keep moving!

World's Pull	**Kingdom of Darkness' Pull**	**Kingdom of God's Pull**
Gravity	Temptation	Trust

As a leader, a creative and as a prophetic model, there are many forces out there that are going to compete for your gift, your attention and your heart. If you're going to be effective, if you're going to be successful in your endeavors and if you're going to be a force to be reckoned with, you will have to learn how to defy gravity. You defy gravity by becoming gravity! Gravity keeps all things centered around the sun. Your job is to keep everyone centered around the Son of God! This is why He said in John 12:32, "And I, if I be lifted up from the earth, will draw all men unto me." Your assignment is to lift Him up in everything that you do! And if you can't lift Him up in it, don't do it! It's that simple!

Prophetic Activation

Find three black holes in your life and pull yourself out of them! Whether it's a bad relationship or a debt that you owe, today is your day for deliverance! Draw up a plan and start pulling yourself out of these black holes; do this every day until you're free! Don't get sucked back in!

Mission Ten

Blast Off!

Prophetic Study Guide

The next few pages are for studying only. You can use them as activation tools as well.

Memory Card

The information on the next two pages is strictly for studying. Every prophet or prophetic model should familiarize himself or herself with the information below. Study these chart and test your memory on the activation.

Major Prophets of the Bible

Isaiah	Jeremiah	Ezekiel	Daniel

Minor Prophets of the Bible

Hosea	Joel	Amos	Obadiah
Jonah	Micah	Nahum	Habakkuk
Zephaniah	Haggai	Zechariah	Malachi

Books in the Bible

Genesis	2 Kings	Isaiah	Nahum	Romans	Titus
Exodus	1 Chronicles	Jeremiah	Habakkuk	1 Corinthians	Philemon
Leviticus	2 Chronicles	Lamentations	Zephaniah	2 Corinthians	Hebrews
Numbers	Ezra	Ezekiel	Haggai	Galatians	James
Deuteronomy	Nehemiah	Daniel	Zechariah	Ephesians	1 Peter
Joshua	Esther	Hosea	Malachi	Philippians	2 Peter
Judges	Job	Joel	Matthew	Colossians	1 John
Ruth	Psalms	Amos	Mark	1 Thessalonians	2 John
1 Samuel	Proverbs	Obadiah	Luke	2 Thessalonians	3 John
2 Samuel	Ecclesiastes	Jonah	John	1 Timothy	Jude
1 Kings	Solomon	Micah	Acts	2 Timothy	Revelation

Prophetesses in the Bible

Please note that these are the women who were specifically called prophets in the Bible. Many would agree that there were more mentioned.

Miriam	**Huldah**	**Anna**
Exodus 15:20	2 Kings 22:14	Luke 2:36-38
Deborah	**Isaiah's Wife**	**Philip's Four Daughters**
Judges 4:4	Isaiah 8:3	Acts 21:8-9

Other women considered to be prophets, but not necessarily mentioned as prophets in the Bible are:

More Female Prophets	Hannah	Elisabeth
Rachel	Abigail	Mary (Mother of Jesus)

12 Tribes in the Bible			
Reuben	Judah	Dan	Asher
Simeon	Issachar	Naphtali	Joseph
Levi	Zebulon	Gad	Benjamin

12 Disciples of Jesus			
Bartholomew	John	Matthew	Philip
James (Son of Zebedee)	Judas Iscariot	Matthias	Simon the Zealot
James (Son of Alpheus)	Jude	Simon Peter	Thomas

7 Churches of Asia	Pergamum	Thyatira	Philadelphia
Ephesus	Smyrna	Sardis	Laodiciea

Prophetic Study Guide

Memory Card Activation

Test your knowledge! Fill in all of the slots below. No cheating!

Major Prophets of the Bible

Minor Prophets of the Bible

Books in the Bible

Prophetic Study Guide

Prophetesses in the Bible

Please note that these are the women who were specifically called prophets in the Bible. Many would agree that there were more mentioned.

Other women considered to be prophets, but not necessarily mentioned as prophets in the Bible are:

More Female Prophets		
		Mary (Mother of Jesus)

12 Tribes in the Bible			

12 Disciples of Jesus			

7 Churches of Asia			

Prophetic Study Guide

Prophetic Functions Challenge

Review the Prophetic Functions chart below. Highlight every function that you've manifested in your life. Also, draw a circle around the functions you believe you're assigned to operate in. Lastly, consider the people you are closest with. What are their prophetic functions, and how do they compliment or constrict you?

Activator	Decoder	Hearer	Nurturer	Scribe
Advisor	Defender	Heart of God	Orator	Seer
Advocate	Deliverer	Herald	Partisan	Servant
Altar Builder	Designer	Incubator	Pattern	Sharer
Analyzer	Devotee	Influencer	Patron	Sifter
Announcer	Director	Inspirer	Peace-Maker	Son
Arbitrator	Disciple	Instigator	Perceptionist	Smoke Detector
Articulator	Dispatcher	Intercessor	Predictor	Sniper
Backer	Dissector	Interpreter	Preparer	Solutionist
Bearer	Diviner	Interventionist	Preserver	Spark
Birther	Dreamer	Intuitivist	Proclaimer	Spokesman
Builder	Edifier	Judge	Prognosticator	Steward
Calibrator	Expounder	Keeper	Promoter	Supporter
Change Agent	Eyes	Leader	Proponent	Surveyor
Cohort	Face Dweller	Liberator	Protector	Transformer
Commentator	Fire Starter	Linker	Psalmist	Translator
Communicator	Follower	Magi	Reconciler	Truth Specialist
Conformer	Forecaster	Marksman	Releaser	Upholder
Confronter	Foreseer	Mediator	Resolver	Vaticinator
Connector	Forth-teller	Merger	Restorer	Visionary
Consultant	Friend of God	Midwife	Revelator	Warrior
Courier	Futurist	Minstrel	Revolutionist	Watchman
Creator	Glory Carrier	Model	Safeguard	Waterer
Custodian	Guard	Mouthpiece	Salvager	Womb
Decipher	Guide	Negotiator	Satellite	Vindicator

Your Periodic Table

In a lab environment, chemicals are mixed together and their reactions are noted. When two chemicals are incompatible, they are often stored in different sections, and they are rarely mixed together unless the teacher or physicist is conducting an experiment.

List the people in your circle (both good and bad) and note how you commonly react to them. What action will you take (starting today) to ensure that you pull out (or restrict) the potential of that relationship? This information will help you to formulate healthy relationships and reposition the people in your life so that you can maximize your God-given potential!

Individual's Name:	
Your Reaction	Action

Prophetic Study Guide

Individual's Name:	
Your Reaction	Action |roof

Individual's Name:	
Your Reaction	Action

Prophetic Study Guide

Individual's Name:	
Your Reaction	Action

Individual's Name:	
Your Reaction	Action

Prophetic Study Guide

Individual's Name:	
Your Reaction	Action

Individual's Name:	
Your Reaction	Action

Prophetic Study Guide

Individual's Name:	
Your Reaction	Action |―

Individual's Name:	
Your Reaction	Action

Prophetic Study Guide

Individual's Name:	
Your Reaction	Action

Individual's Name:	
Your Reaction	Action

Made in the USA
Coppell, TX
26 April 2020